Memoirs of a Cotton Patch Kid

Stories of Growing Up on a
Small Farm in Arkansas
in the 1930s and 1940s

An Autobiography by
Eufa Marie Eubanks Adkison

HERITAGE BOOKS
2006

HERITAGE BOOKS

AN IMPRINT OF HERITAGE BOOKS, INC.

Books, CDs, and more—Worldwide

For our listing of thousands of titles see our website
at
www.HeritageBooks.com

Published 2006 by
HERITAGE BOOKS, INC.
Publishing Division
65 East Main Street
Westminster, Maryland 21157-5026

Copyright © 2006 Eufa Marie Eubanks Adkison

All rights reserved. No part of this book may be reproduced or transmitted in any form or by any means, electronic or mechanical, including photocopying, recording or by any information storage and retrieval system without written permission from the author, except for the inclusion of brief quotations in a review.

International Standard Book Number: **0-7884-3838-7**

Table of Contents

Acknowledgments v
Introduction vii
1. Cheated Out of Childhood? 1
2. The Three-legged Cow 5
3. The Pump 7
4. Staying at Aunt Jessie's House 9
5. Bitter Weeds 11
6. The Quart of Milk 13
7. Cockleburs 15
8. Willow Switch Tea and Razor Strap Soup 17
9. The Tadpole Pond 19
10. Kilroy Was Here 21
11. Bumblebees and Hollyhocks 25
12. Wild Green Onions 27
13. The Mystery of the Missing Washcloths 31
14. Beehives and Burned Socks 35
15. Ground-puppies, Toad Frogs, Warts, and Witches 39
16. Coffee Grounds and Grapevines 43
17. Sex, Rabbits, and Violence 47
18. The Watermelon 53
19. Grandpa Eubanks 55
20. Chocolate Pudding and Blackbird Dumplin's 59
21. Mr. Bill, Mrs. Bessie, Leland, and Bea 61
22. The Raft 63
23. The Quicksand Hole 67
24. The Missing Tractor 69
25. World War II 73
26. Turtle Soup, Hominy, and Lye Soap 77
27. Grandpa Martin 81
28. The Mulberry Bush 85
29. Auntie over, Cowboys and Indians 87
30. Rural Electrification Comes to Kinfolks Island 91
31. Cache River 95
32. Jones Ridge Cemetery 99
33. Flowers of the Field 103
34. Delaplaine, Arkansas, Population 243 107
Poem: Then and Now 110

List of Illustrations

Eufa, Bub, Alma, Betty, Cousin Barbara, and Joyce,
  the original Cotton Patch Kids, about 1944 or 1945 viii
Bub age 1, Eufa age 3, Esther age 11, by a cotton patch in 1936;
  Mama, Bub, Aunt Tildie and Eufa, 1935 4
Eufa, Mama; Daddy, Betty, Joyce, and Bub, 1939 .... facing page 8
Orville and Uncle Isaac; Uncle Isaac, Barbara and
  Aunt Jessie in our yard, about 1941 .... facing page 9
Eufa in our back yard, probably age 15; Eufa being silly, 1948;
  Eufa, our muddy yard, 1947 23
Mama, Alma, Eufa, Betty, Bub, Aunt Tildie, and Joyce at Aunt Jessie's
  house with the morning glory vines and bumblebees 24
Aunt Tildie and Rover, Esther and Spot by the corner of our house, 1941;
  Eufa (about age ten), Mama, Alma, Joyce, Betty, and Bub 30
Eufa's brother Don, age 1; Eufa's sister Noma Lou, age 3, 1948;
  cousins Billy Wayne and George Mack Clark, ages 2 and 4 38
Brownie School students, 1946 46
Wayne Lyons, 1947; cousin Barbara; Eufa and Regina Reynolds, age
  thirteen; Aunt Tildie doing laundry; Eufa and Noma Lou, 1946 51
Eufa's grandpa, Mack Eubanks, about 1956 57
Kids in the cotton wagon, 1949; a family reunion about 1947 66
Eufa and the tractor;
  Daddy, in 1955, in the living room of our old house;
  Family photo, everyone except Betty and Aunt Tildie 71
Joyce, Betty, Noma Lou and Alma, about 1950;
  Eufa and Laura Harlan going fishing, 1949;
  Betty and Joyce in their cotton picking clothes, 1949 76
Joyce, Alma, Noma Lou, Don and our cousin Anna May Pitcher, 1950;
  Joyce, Eufa, Alma, 1952; Eufa's sister Betty (left) and Eufa, 1949;
  Laura Harlan (the preacher's daughter), Eufa and
  Eufa's little brother, Don, 1950 84
Left to right: cousin Barbara, sister Betty, Eufa, cousin Josalee, sister
  Joyce, and sister Alma, 1947 94
The churchhouse we built between our place and Delaplaine, Arkansas;
  Uncle Isaac and Aunt Jessie, 1949;
  A group of people going to church, 1946 106

Acknowledgments

I want to thank my sister, Joyce, for driving me around the old places; my sister, Noma Lou, for her poem; my friend, Helen, for her encouragement; my husband, Albert, for his patience; and my daughter-in-law Nellie for typing the first draft of my manuscript.

Introduction

Did you ever wonder what your life would have been like if you had been born at a different place and time? Or, have you ever wished you were someone else?

I was born in July 1933 in Beech Grove, Arkansas, in the middle of the Great Depression years, the first of seven kids born to Emery and Sadie Eubanks.

My first memories are of cotton patches and lots of water. I am running through those cotton fields beside an ole collie dog, watching my dad plow those fields behind two old work horses.

Everyone I knew worked in the cotton fields; it was the only world I knew. As a kid, I thought everyone did the same things. Of course the only people I knew were relatives, and they all farmed.

During the 1930s, '40s, and '50s, everything around Delaplaine, Arkansas, was about cotton patches and the old Cache River drainage ditch.

These little stories are some of my memories from growing up there in a little place in northeastern Arkansas, called the Cache River bottom lands, of which, my family's little piece of that land was called Kinfolks Island.

Eufa, Bub, Alma, on stump. Betty, Cousin Barbara, Joyce.
The original Cotton Patch Kids, about 1944 or 1945.

- 1 -

Cheated Out of Childhood?

When I was a kid, every time I even thought about the sun it would throw a handful of freckles in my face. You know what they say, "Ignorance is bliss." It was surely true for me, anyway.

I was pretty happy as a child: freckles, stringy dishwater blond hair, knobby knees, buckteeth and all those things the family tree deals you. All we knew anything about was working our butts off in the cotton fields, trying to eke out a living for ten people on thirty-seven acres of swampland overrun with mud, mosquitoes, and crabgrass. (That would surely make any smart kid happy and carefree.) Oh! Starting school was a rude awakening for me, except I tried not to wake up for about the first three years of it. That's almost as long as I got to go.

I guess I was six years old when I was first put on that thing they called a school bus; that was the same year my sister Joyce was born. I remember that day in August. My grandma came to our house. I remember Mama washing her feet and putting on a gown. I thought it was strange for Mama to do that in the middle of the afternoon. I thought she was sick and I was scared, but Aunt Tildie took me and we went to a neighbor's house and I played with their kids awhile. Then Aunt Tildie came back and got us, as my brother and younger sister, Betty, were there too. When we got home I was glad to see Mama was OK, and was sitting up in the bed holding a little baby with black hair and dimples. That made four kids; I was the oldest.

At that time we were living on a farm three miles west of Delaplaine owned by a man Daddy called "Old Auger Eye." He was a German man and he had a glass eye, hence the nickname. Daddy sharecropped for him. That in itself was a bad scene as sharecropping meant that we did all the work and Old Auger Eye got the entire share.

Anyway, that was the summer of 1939 and I was old enough to start to school. School started in July and went through August. Then we got out for three or four months to pick cotton. We usually picked cotton until sometime around the middle of November, but sometimes until December, or when the water got up too high and all the cotton bolls fell off and rotted. Then we went to school until April or May, and then it was time to start working all over again. That meant for us kids, Aunt Tildie, and sometimes Mama, to get our cotton hoes sharpened and go hoe the weeds and grass from around the little cotton plants. Ever try doing that for a couple of months straight?

Some years it rained so much Daddy didn't get the crops planted on time. When it rained a lot in February the old drainage ditch would flood, water would get out all over the fields and in our yard, and it went away very slowly. Us kids would have to wear knee boots (made out of rubber) to school. We would carry our shoes and change when we got to the schoolhouse porch.

This was after we moved. Daddy bought the thirty-seven acres over where my Aunt Jessie (Mama's sister) and Uncle Isaac (Dad's brother) lived, three miles east of Delaplaine. My dad built a two-room house out of logs he had cut up and taken to a sawmill where he had boards made out of them. Us kids thought that it was the grandest house ever; it smelled so good the day we moved into it. I remember the first night we spent there. We went to Uncle Isaac's house first and had to walk the rest of the way. It wasn't far but there was a big mud puddle between our place and Uncle Isaac's. I remember Uncle Isaac carrying me on his back across the water and mud holes.

Our place was still just made up of woods and old sloughs with big old cypress trees and stumps. Daddy, us kids and Aunt Tildie (I'll tell you about her later) got to work clearing all that up so Daddy could plant cotton that spring; I think he got to plant about five acres that year, which was 1940. We cleared a place for a garden: a vegetable garden, of course. We had some chickens and an ole milk cow. We nearly always ate taters and beans for dinner, beans and taters for supper, and biscuits and gravy for breakfast. Sometimes we would find enough eggs for breakfast if some animal or big black chicken snake didn't find them first. I don't know what we had more of, chickens or snakes.

Sometimes we had chicken and dumplings for dinner on Sunday (then, it was on Sunday). That was before the church thing got started. After that the chicken and dumplings were on Saturday. We would come home after church and run down an ole hen and Mama would wring its neck off and cook dinner for at least twelve people. My aunts would send their kids over to play at our house. There were so many of us anyway, what did a few more matter? I guess that was their way of thinking. And if it weren't the cousins, the preacher and his family would be invited over, or most likely invite themselves. But that was a few years before 1940. Before that time we didn't go to church, or anywhere else except the cotton fields and school when we didn't have to work, which wasn't very often.

When I was thirteen I could pick a nine-foot cotton sack full of cotton. I could pick it up and throw it over my shoulder, carry it a quarter of a mile to where the wagon was parked, and put it on the scales. It might weigh seventy pounds. I would hand it up to someone in the wagon. They would shake all the cotton out and then throw the empty sack back down to me. I would walk back to the field and pick cotton again until noon, carry that sack to the wagon—it might weigh fifty pounds or more—then I could eat lunch before going back to the cotton field and working until sundown.

I know now why the water moccasin snakes, the loggerhead turtles and the mosquitoes didn't eat us kids: we were too fast and too tough. Also, there were a lot of guardian angels flying around there in those days.

Bub age 1, Eufa age 3, Esther age 11,
taken by a cotton patch in 1936

Mama holding Bub,
Aunt Tildie with Eufa standing in front of her, 1935

The Three-legged Cow

I don't remember how that old three-legged iron cow came to be. I think Daddy found her while he was plowing the fields for corn and cotton.

There were seven of us kids and we didn't have much in the way of what kids nowadays think of as toys. In fact, the only toys we had were the ones we made ourselves, like corncob dolls and toy guns we whittled out of an old board or a stick, or slingshots made from forked sticks from a hickory tree (that is the best kind), tongues from old leather shoes, and pieces of old inner tubes (that was before tubeless tires). My grandpa had an ole Model T car, so sometimes we could get an old inner tube from him. The tubes usually had so many patches on them it was hard to find a strip long enough for our slingshots. We had a few old tin cans, some oyster shells, broken dishes, and stuff like that. We would make play houses and play stores and fill them up with those kinds of things, and one of those things was the old toy iron cow with one leg missing that Daddy found while plowing the land.

The land Daddy farmed was called bottom land, or swamp land. But there were places on the land where it was kind of sandy and had little mounds, or "hills," as us kids called them.

We found lots of Indian arrowheads there; you know, the spearheads Indians used to make out of stone or flint and lash them to their arrows.

I think some Indian tribe must have lived on the land a long time before we moved there and farmed it. Maybe those mounds were burial grounds. But as a kid I never knew anything about that. I didn't know until just recently that I'm enough Cherokee Indian to get a membership card and a blood degree certificate from the Cherokee tribe. My Great

Grandfather and Grandfather Martins' names are on the Dawes Rolls at Tahlequah, Oklahoma.

    I guess you are wondering what the heck that has to do with an old toy iron, or stone, three-legged cow we used to play with. Well, maybe nothing at all. But let's go back there to the place where I was a kid and know the things I know now, like all the things about the Indians and their ways and my own heritage. I remember one summer day I was playing in my play store by myself (which is strange anyway, because with four sisters and two brothers you don't often play by yourself) and no one else was outside playing. I was placing things around the store like I thought they should be placed and I remember picking up the old three-legged cow. I dropped her and when I stooped down to pick her up...she wasn't there. Not on the ground or anywhere else. I had the strangest feeling, and the feeling got even stranger, when I thought I heard a small faint giggle right beside me. I looked all around me but no one else was in sight and neither was that old three-legged cow.

    What do you think happened to it?

    I told my sisters and brothers about losing it and they all looked for her too.

    But no one ever saw that old toy iron cow ever again.

    Or did we?!?

    During this same period of time we had an ole milk cow we used to call Molly. I think she was a Jersey milk cow. Anyway, in the spring of the next year ole Molly gave birth to a heifer calf. My dad said that it was a pretty rusty red in color, but it was deformed and that is why it didn't live.

    You see, it only had *three legs!*

The Pump

June in the lowlands of northeastern Arkansas is like being in the Tropics. It gets so hot and humid, that my dad used to say, "The air is so humid you can slice it with a knife."

If you were me in the 1940s, you got up at sunrise, put on your overalls and a bonnet or big straw hat and a pair of gloves, if you are lucky enough to own a pair. Then you and your brother Bub, sisters Betty and Joyce, and your cousin Barbara and of course Aunt Tildie, headed out for what seemed like a mile walk to the cotton patch on Uncle Isaac's farm. That is where you would be chopping cotton that day. By the time you got there you were already hot, sweaty and not a bit happy; but, you were a kid and you did what your dad told you to do. Besides, you already knew, if you didn't work, you didn't eat.

This was my life in the 1940s. Us kids and Aunt Tildie chopped the cotton in the spring, and Daddy and Uncle Isaac plowed it with a team of ole stubborn mules.

Maybe you are wondering what it meant to chop cotton. I'm pretty sure you are wondering that if you are under fifty years old. Well! To chop cotton, or hoe cotton, you take a cotton hoe. A cotton hoe is about the same as a garden hoe. You chop a place the width of the hoe and leave two little cotton plants standing, then you chop out all the weeds and grass from around the baby cotton plants.

The rows are about a quarter of a mile long. To me, at that age, they seemed to go on forever.

Mama would bring us some lunch at noon, or thereabouts. It would usually consist of soup-beans and fried taters and maybe tomatoes out of the garden, if she had time to go to the garden and pick them. On this very hot humid morning with the sun beating on our heads and backs, it sure made us look forward to seeing Mama and the beans and taters. We didn't bring something to drink because on this particular cotton patch there was a water well with an old pump so we could always take a break and go to the pump for a drink. Have you ever gotten a drink from an old water pump in the middle of June, in the middle of a cotton patch? Bet you haven't. It's very nice when the pump will work. You pull the handle up and down a couple of times and out comes the water clear and cold. Right? Wrong! On this day, the darn thing had lost its prime, or in other words, the water had gone down so far in the pipe and the suction cup had dried out, so the water couldn't be pumped up.

What did we do?

We were very hot and thirsty. Mama was nowhere to be seen. We were a mile from our house and the nearest water was in a patch of woods down the side of the cotton field.

We could go there to use the *bathroom*. We decided to do just that, and besides it was a lot cooler there in the woods.

Us girls went first. There were some old rusty tin cans and things someone had dumped there in the woods. Soooo…we used one of them for a potty. We all peed in the old rusty can. We then started back to the cotton patch when we saw Bub coming down to the woods. We had a bright idea! Bub, we said, you pee in the can too. We took it to the pump and primed the pump with the pee. After we pumped it for several minutes, we get a nice stream of cool water and we all had a drink.

I guess today you would call that recycling!

Then Aunt Tildie came and said, "Well, I see you got the pump primed," as she was getting herself a drink. Then she looked at us kids and asked, "Where did you get water to prime the pump?"

Us kids said in one voice, "In the woods."

This photo was taken on the sharecropper's farm in 1939, just before we moved to the thirty-seven-acre farm.
Eufa standing in from of Mama; Daddy sitting, holding Betty and Joyce; Bub standing by.

Orville and Uncle Isaac
(the way it was)

Uncle Isaac, holding Barbara; Aunt Jessie, standing, taken in our yard, old log barn in background, about 1941

- 4 -

Staying at Aunt Jessie's House

Just before we moved over on Kinfolks Island in 1939, to our thirty-seven acres by Uncle Isaac's and Aunt Jessie's place, I was sent to stay with them and go to school with my cousin, Esther. I was almost seven and she was about fourteen. My cousin Barbara (Esther's sister) was just a baby, or toddler.

I hated being sent there. I didn't like to go to school with Esther and she didn't like to go with me either. To her I was a tag-along and a nuisance. I cried a lot. But then I hit on what I thought was a new idea. I'd get sick and Mama would have to come to Aunt Jessie's and get me and take me back home with her. Well, I decided to play sick the very next day. Aunt Jessie sent word to Mama that I was sick and she came to see about me. She gave me a dose of senna tea and in a little while it kicked in. I found a toilet, underneath the front porch of Aunt Jessie's house. There I could hear Mama and Aunt Jessie talking as I was doing my thing from the senna tea under the porch. I heard Mama say to Aunt Jessie, "I know she ain't sick; but now she will remember lying and will know what will happen to her if she does it again." She was right; that senna tea is awful. I think they knew where I was and that I could hear them talk. I never forgot that and never pretended to be sick again in order to get out of something I didn't want to do. It didn't do any good with my mama; it seemed she knew everything. She would always tell us, she had "eyes in the back of her head." We knew it was so.

That same weekend Daddy came and took me home; but in a few days we loaded up all our belongings and headed out down through the woods, down the bank of Cache River, and were soon back at Aunt Jessie's and Uncle Isaac's house. I didn't realize Daddy had our house finished and we were going to be living in it. I was thinking I'd have to stay at Aunt Jessie's again and go to school with Esther, and Aunt Jessie would make us peanut butter and crackers (with a little sugar on) for our sandwiches for our school lunches. I hated those. That's probably why Mama figured I needed the senna tea.

I don't know how my cousin Barbara ever started walking, because Aunt Jessie would put so many cloth didies (diapers) on her at night, her little short fat legs would be sticking out sideways. It's a wonder her hips didn't get out of joint! There were no plastic pants back then, so in order to keep babies dry at night, they had to wear a lot of padding, mostly made out of feed and flour sacks that had been bleached out white with plenty of lye soap. You wouldn't think that would be a memory a seven-year-old would end up keeping for over sixty years, would you?

From that time until I was grown, Barbara was just like one of my sisters. We were always together; she and my sister Betty were about the same age. Joyce was two years younger than them. I remember those three girls would get into a fight and bite each other. In order to try to solve the biting problem, either my mama or Aunt Jessie would bite them back on the arm. They thought that that would show the girls how badly it hurt to be bitten (like they shouldn't have already known). Sometimes when I think of some of the things that went on back then, I think maybe my mama and aunts were just a little bit sadistic. Really, I think it came from my Grandpa Martin. He did mean things to his kids (my mom and aunts) when they were growing up. Mama would tell stories about the things he did to them, like locking them up in dark cellars, or tying them to the porch post and making them stay there all day without food. I knew my grandpa. I believe what she told was true.

Bitter Weeds

Do you have a lawnmower? Do you have to mow the lawn?

When I was a kid there weren't any lawnmowers, or if there were any, we didn't know anything about them and couldn't have owned one even if we *had* known about them. All our yard had in it were weeds and kids anyway; I don't know which there were more of, either.

When someone would ask Mama, "How are all the kids?" all I remember her saying was, "Growing like weeds."

Well, getting back to mowing our yard. We, or me, my brother Bub, and two of my sisters who were big enough at the time, would take garden hoes and chop down all the weeds in the yard and when we got done all that was left was the bare ground. The bare ground mostly turned to dust, except when it rained, which was quite often where we lived, being in the lowlands in northeastern Arkansas, the flood lands of the Cache River. Well, the lawn then turned into a mud puddle. We had to put logs all around in order to walk on it.

Sometimes it rained so much the yard was like a lake. There would be water all the way up to where our pump was on a little knoll. We would have to go up there to get water to drink and use for cooking and everything else in the house. It was like the saying, "Water, water everywhere but nary a drop to drink." And to get the water to drink we had to put logs all the way to the pump or wade in the floodwaters to get to the pump. I've always thought the reason why my arms are so long is because I carried so many buckets of water across the foot logs to the house. I had to carry two at the same time to keep my balance or else I'd end up with more water than I wanted.

When the floodwaters went away the weeds would come back, unless it was wintertime, then it all froze over and we could skate on it. But don't try to carry buckets of water while skating on ice; that doesn't work well at all!

Sometimes the floodwaters would get so deep we would put our water buckets in a boat and go get drinking water and paddle the boat right up on the front porch.

When it was flooded, we would go through the woods in the boat for half a mile to catch the school bus over on Arnolds Hill. Sometimes it would be raining too. It was a lot of fun to be in a boat with water everywhere and have it raining on your head. When we got on the bus all the kids would ask us if we swam all the way to catch the bus; they would say that we really must have wanted to go to school badly.

This was after we started going to school "in town;" that's what we considered the school at Delaplaine, Arkansas. Delaplaine wasn't much in the way of a town; the school was the largest building there, except for the cotton gin. The cotton gin was where Daddy sold the cotton we picked. They processed it and put it into big bales and then put the bales on the trains to send to big city factories, which turned the cotton into cloth for clothes and more cotton sacks for us to put cotton into.

Bitter weeds? Don't know if the bitter weeds were the ones we chopped down, or if us kids grew up to be the bitter weeds. I look back on those days now and I'm not feeling bitter at all, so I guess it was really the weeds in the lawn with the bitter tasting and smelling little yellow flowers.

The cows liked to eat them, but when you drank the milk from the cows, Yuck! Should that have left a bitter taste in your memory?

Oh! And biscuits and butter made with the milk from the bitter weed-eating cows. Well you guessed it, they were bitter too!

And in my memory—I can taste it still, sixty years later.

The Quart of Milk

"Here! You carry it."

"No! I carried it yesterday!"

"No you didn't. I did. Besides you're the biggest and Mama said for you to do it."

My brother always threw the jar of milk at me and I always threw it back to him as we walked across Mr. and Mrs. Moore's plowed cotton field on our way to school.

We had to walk two miles to get to the one-room schoolhouse and we had to carry our lunches and schoolbooks also. We weren't supposed to walk across anyone's fields but we cut across them anyway. We thought it was closer that way. So we threw the jar of milk for our lunch up and down and across the cotton rows; it's a wonder it wasn't churned to butter by the time we got to school. And the cotton patch didn't fare so well either. And you can guess what us kids looked like, along with what the jar of milk must have looked like. Did you ever walk across a plowed field in the middle of a hot June day in Arkansas?

When the teacher saw us it wasn't hard for her to figure out the problem, especially when she had help from my younger sisters and cousin. Of course, Mama heard all about it. From then on guess who carried the milk and lunches? The oldest kid of course, which was me, because I knew better than to walk across plowed fields and throw jars of milk at my brother.

I was the oldest of seven kids so it was my job to take care of the rest of the kids going to school and coming home. That was the largest part of my education, because girls didn't need a lot of book learning; all they needed to know was how to spell, write their names, know their ABCs, and that "one and one makes three or four or how ever many more came along" (my parents' thoughts on school for girls). Going to that one-room school until I was through the fifth grade and was fourteen years old was most of my book learning. After that year the one-room school was consolidated into the big school at Delaplaine, the Town School. I went to the Town School for two more years, until 1951. That was the extent of my book learning until I was fifty-five years old. Then in 1989, I took a GED course and got my diploma saying I was a high school graduate; and I still know how to toss a mean jar of milk.

Cockleburs

Get your head out of the clouds; stop counting birds; get your back bent over that row and your head in those cotton stalks.

It's the middle of the afternoon on a late September day. You have been in this cotton patch since sunup, trying to get a wagonload of cotton picked before sundown. That's what your dad expects from you and your brothers and sisters, and we understand we have to do it. But you are also a kid and you are tired and hot. The sun is beating down on your straw-hat covered head and the flies are buzzing around you trying to get a drink off your sweaty, dirty face.

The cotton stalks here in this patch at the foot of Cache River Ditch are as tall as you are, and the cocklebur stalks are even taller and loaded with cockleburs. If you get your hat knocked off by one of them (while trying to maneuver around the burr stalks to get to some cotton to pick and put in your sack), your hair gets full of cockleburs. It takes you an hour to get them out of your hair when you finally get home at night.

That is after you go and pump buckets of water and carry it to the kitchen and carry in armloads of firewood for the kitchen stove so that Mama can cook supper; then maybe you can take a bath, if you have carried water and filled the number three washtub that morning and let it set in the sun all day to get warm. Maybe by the time you get to use it, three of your younger sisters have beaten you to it. (No "Calgon, take me away" here!) Ouch! OH! What is that sticking to my naked butt? Only cockleburs, the little sisters picked out of their hair while taking a bath and left in the tub *you* filled that morning!

Seems like if there was any justice in the world, you should have gotten to use your water first; after all you are the oldest.

But that wasn't the privilege bestowed on the eldest child in those days; not in my world, not at all.

"Come eat supper," Mama yells, just as I've gotten the burrs picked out of the bath water. Boy, if I don't hurry, there won't be any beans and taters and cornbread left.

Now wash the dishes and go to bed, so you can get up with the sun in the morning and go pick some more cotton. Well at least not in that patch with the cockleburs. That is one thing to be thankful for; that patch has been picked already. In about a week we will have to do it again though and there will be even more cockleburs. They just keep making more, just like the cotton stalks right up until it gets to be freezing cold in the middle of November. Believe me by that time you are ready for everything to freeze.

Then you can go back to school. It isn't even a chore to walk the two miles through the mud and water to get to school after you have been picking cotton every day for the past three months. In fact, it's a blessing. Your fingers can get well and you can finally get all the cockleburs out of your hair; but not the freckles off your face.

I tried everything I could think of and everything anyone told me to do to get rid of them, but to this day the freckles and a few other things are still with me, sixty-odd years later.

Willow Switch Tea and Razor Strap Soup

We had our own folk remedies for attention deficit disorder, hyperactivity, bipolar syndrome, and other childhood ailments.

When I was a kid no one ever heard of those kinds of disorders or afflictions, because back then parents believed in plenty of willow switches, and Daddy's razor strap wasn't used just to sharpen his double-edged razor. It was also use to warm up kids' behinds when they got all disorganized and out of sorts, just like chicken soup would do for a bad cold.

When kids had thoughts and actions that weren't normal for children, well, it was said they needed "a dose of hickory tea." In our neck of the woods, this meant willow switch tea, because that bush was real handy for Mama to get the limbs needed to give us a dose. And it didn't do any good to say, you didn't want it and try to run away, as she would say, "You have to sleep sometime." And you would end up getting a rude awakening, plus a double dose of the willow switch tea on your behind.

Willow switch tea is nasty tasting and stings like a bee and leaves long-lasting red welts across your butt and in your mind.

There were other kinds of remedies for all kinds of ailments or disorders, like if you got intestinal worms, you got a teaspoon full of sugar with three drops of turpentine on it; then the next day you got a big dose of senna tea. In a few hours you would be in the outhouse or down behind the barn getting rid of your intestinal worm problem. Depending upon how strong the senna tea was, sometimes you thought you were getting rid of all your guts as well.

For earaches, you were sent to find and bring back a dirt daubers' nest. Mama would break open the nest and take out the dirt dauber larva, stick a pin or needle in the tail end of the larva and three or four drops of a pale yellow oily fluid would drop out. She would catch it in a teaspoon and warm it over an old kerosene lamp and drop that dirt dauber oil in our ear, and *voila!* It would stop the earache.

For bad colds and the grippe, Daddy would make a nice cocoa syrup. (Ha, ha!) He also added quinine. I guess his motto was, "What won't kill, will cure."

For sore throats and tonsillitis, Mama made sage tea with honey and alum. You gargled with it, and if you didn't feel better you were so puckered up you couldn't complain for quite a while anyway.

Us kids never were sick very much; anyway we didn't go around complaining about it. We figured the cure was worse than the disease.

Oh! Guess I never mentioned that our mom was half Cherokee Indian, did I? Other half Black Dutch. Dad was English and Irish; I suppose that makes me a "Heinz fifty-seven??"

The Tadpole Pond

> At goldenrod and aster time
> The fairies near our pool
> Put on their freshly laundered things
> And fluttered off to school.
> They sat at little toadstool desks
> And did their fairy sums
> And learned to color autumn leaves
> Before the Frost King comes.
>
> —*unknown*

I don't know the author of that little poem. I learned it by memory when I was in the third grade; it was in an old book in our library at the one-room schoolhouse. Our library was a metal cabinet with four shelves in the corner at the back of the room.

By the time I finished fifth grade I had read all the books on those shelves, but that is the only poem I remember from then. I guess it was because I too had a fairy pool; it was a natural pond in the woods between our house and Grandma and Orville's. After we chopped cotton for them in the spring, we would cut through those woods on our way home at night, or just before it got dark. There must have been hundreds of frogs in that small pond. We would watch the frogs lay their eggs. Then we would go back every evening to see them hatch into tadpoles and then grow into tiny frogs. There were also a million dragonflies sitting around on the reeds at the edge of the water. I thought they were the fairies just waiting for the frogs to turn them into princes, just like in the fairytale. I had read that too.

In the summer the pond would almost go dry and the frogs would hop off into the woods. But in the autumn after it rained, the pond would fill up again and the frogs and the dragonflies would return. So every evening on our way home from picking cotton for Grandma we would run through the woods to the pond. I thought I could catch the fairies painting the leaves. I know now that the dragonflies were sitting there waiting to catch a mosquito or a gnat, and the frogs were just discussing where they would hibernate for the long cold winter.

I still like to think that the pond was a fairy pool. Kids have so much more fun than grownups-even kids who have to work hard like I did!

A book and your imagination can take you anywhere you want to go.

- 10 -

Kilroy Was Here

I spent most of my growing-up years on Kinfolks Island. It was called Kinfolks Island by the people at Delaplaine for a good reason I suppose.

Every farm close to ours was owned by a relative.

The first farm across the bridge where the water left the creek that drained off from Cache River, was my Grandma's and Step-grandpa Orville's house; Aunt Mary's and Uncle Ben's place was to the side of the road; then there was Uncle Isaac's and Aunt Jessie's place. Uncle Isaac was Daddy's brother; Aunt Jessie was Mama's sister. That made Esther and Barbara my double cousins. Aunt Mary was also Mama and Aunt Jessie's sister. Aunt Mary had nine kids. Then there was our place. In all there got to be seven of us kids and with Aunt Tildie, Mama's sister who lived with us for as long as I could remember, that made a pretty big bunch of cotton-picking kids.

When we caught up on our cotton picking for Daddy, we would go to Grandma's or one of the uncles' and pick cotton for them. When we did that we got paid for the pounds of cotton we picked. In a day's time, if you worked real hard you could pick two hundred pounds, or thereabout. You got paid three dollars for a hundred pounds, so if you were lucky, or a good cotton-picking kid, you could make five or six dollars a day! Usually we were allowed to keep that money to buy our school clothes for the fall and winter. Once or twice in the fall we could go to the city (which was Paragould, Arkansas) and shop for winter clothes and shoes. Grandma and Orville would take us; they were the only ones who owned a car back then. It was an old Model T. Grandma and Orville would fuss and quarrel all the way there and all the time we were shopping, and all the way back again, which was thirty miles each way. Orville drove about twenty-five or thirty miles an hour; sometimes I didn't think we would make it up Pine Hill.

Well, we did make it, with Grandma, Orville, Aunt Tildie, and my sisters, Betty and Joyce. Aunt Tildie helped them buy their shoes and clothes. Grandma was too busy fussing at Orville about whether he might be looking at another woman. You see, he was twenty years younger than Grandma, and she was a very jealous-hearted person. I was fourteen that year so I got to do my own shopping and I found a pair of jeans I thought were the greatest, or as kids would say nowadays, "they were to die for." At fourteen you like funky clothes no matter if you are a cotton-patch kid or not. The jeans were a new and an "in thing," for lack of a better phrase. They were blue and had graffiti all over them. They had big red lips on them and sayings of the time; and one of the sayings was "Kilroy was Here." Well! I bought them. They cost a day's worth of cotton picking.

Well, the first day of school I put on those jeans. But Daddy saw me as I started out the door and said, "Take those things off; you are not going any place in that." Oh! I cried a lot, but I changed clothes. We knew better than to argue with our parents, especially with Daddy. When I got home Mama and Aunt Tildie had been doing laundry. They washed the "Kilroy was Here" jeans in a kettle with boiling water and lye soap. Almost all the graffiti was washed out; Kilroy was not there any more. So Mama let me wear the jeans. Daddy never said anything else about them, but I heard him telling Mama, "as long as we were in his house putting our feet under his table, we would go by his rules, no matter if we were forty years old."

I never bought any more funky clothes...that year at least.

Me (Eufa) in our back yard, probably age 15

Me being silly trying to entertain my little brother and sister, 1948

Me, our muddy yard, 1947

Mama holding Alma; Eufa and Betty standing in front; Bub, Aunt Tildie, and Joyce standing in front of her at Aunt Jessie's house with the morning glory vines and bumblebees.

- 11 -

Bumblebees and Hollyhocks

Uncle Isaac and Aunt Jessie's house was an old three-room (*not* three-bedroom) farmhouse with a big front porch with morning glories growing all over it and there was an old storm cellar in the yard. The cellar had a mound of dirt on top of it and all around. Aunt Jessie would plant flowers all over it; she had larkspurs, butterfingers, but mostly, hollyhocks. All us kids loved to play in their yard, which didn't please her at all; but it did her daughter, Barbara. They only had two kids. Esther was older than me by seven years and she was ten or eleven years older than Barbara. Esther didn't play with us younger kids, so Barbara was always with us: at our house, in the cotton patch, in the woods, at the old sloughs fishing, or going to school. Sometimes Aunt Jessie would have to let us all play at her house or else Barbara would cry.

On a hot summer day we were all there in their yard and the bumblebees were there, as they loved that yard too, especially because of the hollyhocks. The bees would go inside the blossoms and get pollen all over their legs and mouths until they could barely fly off. We would sneak up on them and close the blossoms around the bumblebees and take them to a big jar we had sitting on the front porch and shake the bees out into the jar and cover it with a lid, sometimes we would run after the bees when they would fly off and we would swat them with sticks. It only knocked them unconscious. We then could pick them up by their wings and put them in the jar. Well, on this day we had a whole jar full of bees. Then Mama yelled at us to come on, we had chores to do; so off we ran forgetting to let the bumblebees loose.

I guess no one noticed them until the next morning, when Uncle Isaac got up and went out on the porch to pee. (He didn't take time to put on his shoes and walk down the path to the outhouse, just went out on the porch to pee.) Well! He found the bumblebees. He stubbed his bare toes on the jar, knocking it over. The lid came off and for sure the bees were fighting mad and took it out on Uncle Isaac's bare feet. Oh, and he was allergic to bee stings, too. (He only had one good eye; that was because a honeybee had stung him on the other eye a long time before.) Boy, he was yelling and hollering and we could hear him all the way to our house. They put a lot of vinegar and baking soda on the stings and he was OK. I think his foot did better than our behinds; it wasn't vinegar and baking soda that was applied to our butts. We got willow switch tea. And no more catching bumblebees and putting them in jars; we didn't even get to play in his yard for a long time after that.

From then on we only caught fireflies and put them in jars. Oh, yeah, and horseflies. We stuck white chicken feathers in their tails and watched them fly off into the twilight.

These were the things kids did before television and video games. We made up our own games and sometimes they weren't so nice either. But we never gave a thought that what we were doing to the bumblebees and horseflies was considered by some people to be cruel.

Wild Green Onions

I've heard it said, "You can't go home again."
But for me that's not so true
Because to go there, all I have to do,
Is close my eyes, and in my heart and mind,
I go back to a place and time
When I was eight or nine.
I can sit at the bottom of a riverbank
Beneath some willow trees—
I have cold biscuits in a paper bag,
And there growing all around
Are wild green onions to eat with them.
And I am surely home again.
This only works with one mode
Of transportation though.

—*Eufa Eubanks Adkison*

When us kids would come home from school in the late afternoon, we were just like all kids; we were hungry. But the differences between back then and now are enormous in other ways. When we got home Mama was always there. We had no television or video games. We had a radio, though. Mostly Daddy listened to ballgames or the news, and sometimes we got to listen to the radio program, Superman. Mostly we got told to go outside and play. So we'd grab some cold biscuits that had been left over from breakfast and we'd go down by the river and eat our snack of biscuits with wild green onions. We could catch some small frogs, or dig a worm and set out our fishing poles. We could catch some fish and take them home to clean them. ("If you catch them you clean them," was Mama's motto.) Then Mama would cook them for supper. We ate a lot of fish, squirrels, and wild ducks. When

Daddy wasn't working in the fields, or cutting ties for the railroad, he was fishing and hunting. But it wasn't for sport; it was to put food on the table. We didn't go to the grocery stores very often. Our school snacks weren't potato chips and Twinkies®; I didn't even know there were such things back then.

Did you ever scale a fish, pick feathers off a wild duck, or skin a squirrel when you were a kid? Knowing how to do that meant that you were going to have something to eat for supper or else you went to bed hungry. And scaling, skinning and picking wasn't all you needed to know. You also had to take the guts out of the animal or bird and cut up the meat. Oh! We also killed and processed our own hogs. When I was real small, that would scare the pee out of me. I always hated that time of the year, especially after I got big enough to help with it. Aren't you glad you don't have to get your ham sandwich that way, or your bacon to go with your eggs?

I guess we were lucky in a way though, because we knew some people that lived down Cache River who didn't even have that much, or maybe they didn't know how to work and provide for it. Sometimes for lunch they would have the meat they brought to school; it would be an old blue crane they had killed and cooked. I think that would be worse than eating blackbird dumplings.

Those kids always wanted us to go home with them to stay the night. One time my sister, Betty, went and she had to sleep with their daughter. Well, Betty got the seven-year itch, and of course she gave it to all of us too. Was that ever a mess! Daddy went to see ole Doc Hutchens at Delaplaine and got some stuff to get rid of the itch. It was called Sitiside, and it smelled like a skunk with a fit. We had to take a bath and put that stuff all over ourselves and wait thirty minutes, then take another bath. And this was in the wintertime. Think of all the water we had to pump and carry and heat on the old wood-burning stove. Then think of ten people having to take baths in a number three washtub in January in front of the old woodstove. Think of them doing that twice in one night, while all the time the skunk smell permeated the whole house. Oh! We had to do this all again the next week; but we got over the seven-year itch in two weeks. Betty never stayed over night with her friend Dennese again. We all told her what would happen if she did. I don't know what could have been worse than that itch, but she thought we would figure out something.

Aunt Tildie and Rover; Esther and Spot by the corner of our house, 1941

Eufa, Mama holding Alma, Joyce, Betty, Bub. I was probably ten years old here. Aunt Tildie had an old Kodak camera; she was always taking pictures. She bought film and had the pictures developed with her cotton picking money.

- 13 -

The Mystery of the Missing Washcloths

In February 1947, the year I was fourteen, my baby brother Donald was born. I knew Mama was going to have another baby although she and Aunt Tildie tried very hard to keep us other kids from knowing about it. Back then you didn't tell kids much of anything about grown-up stuff, as they called things like that. At fourteen-and-a-half I was still just a kid (to them anyway.) Of course, I didn't see it that way.

I knew why Mama had gotten fat, and I knew she and Aunt Tildie were sewing baby clothes; they would do most of that while we were gone to school and hide them in an old trunk Aunt Tildie kept her things in. Daddy called it her Hopeless Chest. Aunt Tildie got teased a lot. She was fat and was considered an old maid. She hardly ever had a boyfriend. She had what you would call today, an "attitude."

The night Mama went into labor with Don, Daddy went to tell Grandma and Aunt Jessie to come over. Then he went to Delaplaine and got Doctor Hutchens. Daddy dropped all us kids off at Uncle Isaac's. I didn't want to leave. I wanted to stay and help Mama and see what all the fuss about having a baby was all about, and what the big secret was. But, no, they wouldn't let me stay. I was too young to know those things; of course, it just made me even more curious. Kids today know more about sex when they are ten than I knew when I got married.

I didn't start having my periods until that spring; I was almost fifteen at the time. I remember very well the morning I got up and I'd started my period. I thought I was going to bleed to death, that something was wrong with me. Oh, I'd heard a few things from some of the girls at school about getting the "Curse," and having the cramps, but I really didn't know what they meant. Well! That morning I found out (kind of). I went to the kitchen where Mama was cooking breakfast. Aunt Tildie was there helping her. They asked me what was wrong; they could tell something was because I was crying and scared. I told them. And guess what? Mama just said, "Oh that," and told Aunt Tildie to show me what to do. Guess what that was? Well, she took me to the bedroom, got some white cloth, folded it up, handed me a safety pin and said, "pin that to the inside of your bloomers." She told me that's what girls do when they get to be my age, if not before, and told me I would be all right, that there was nothing wrong with me. That was all the education I got at that time on the subject.

After that I told the younger girls what to expect and, from my experience, what they had to do. Ha!

One time a couple of years later when Betty started having her periods, she never said a word to anyone. A few months later, Mama started fussing about why we didn't have any washcloths and wondering what had happened to all of them. No one knew, nor could we find them anywhere. Until one day Aunt Tildie was looking for a little kitten that had become lost. She thought she heard it meowing underneath the smokehouse, so she got down on her hands and knees and looked underneath the smokehouse. She not only found the kitten, she also discovered the missing washcloths. We came to find out that Betty wasn't using the white cloths for her pads (she didn't want to wash them on laundry day; yes, that is what we had to do back then). Betty just used washcloths and then threw them under the old smokehouse. Mama said she should make her crawl under there and get them all out and wash them herself; but she didn't. I guess she thought they would be in too big of a mess, which was surely true.

After that we discovered there was such a thing as Kotex® and if you were brave enough and had a little money you could go to Delaplaine to Tom Hall's store and buy them. But you know, I'd rather use the rags and wash them as to go to that store and tell Tom Hall what I wanted to buy, because that is what you had to do in order to get them. When you wanted to buy something in his store you would have to tell him what you wanted and he would get them off the shelves behind the counter. Sometimes his mother would run the store so we got brave enough to ask her for the Kotex, or else Mama would tell Daddy to buy them for her and us girls. He would say, "So the girls are out of cereal, huh?" He told Tom Hall one day that he "didn't know what he had to buy more of, food or Kotex." Guess that is why he started calling the sanitary napkins, "cereal." Anyway by that time there were five of us girls and Kotex was cheaper than washcloths. My girls never knew their grandpa but I have told them this story. So guess what they call sanitary napkins? Cereal, of course! Kotex used to come in boxes you know....

Beehives and Burned Socks

By the time I was twelve years old there were at least ten kids from Kinfolks Island walking to Brownie School. They made up about a third of the pupils at the one-room school.

The cousins would all meet at our house, as it was the last house on the way to school. We would all trudge off through the woods like a herd of goats, most of the time through mud and water, for the two miles to school. We had to cross a creek. Daddy had cut a tree down and made it fall across the creek. We had to walk on the foot log in order to get across the creek. Well, it wasn't easy to get our cousin, Barbara, to walk across that foot log; she was kind of a chubby girl and not as agile as the rest of us.

I had the chore of getting her to walk across the creek on the log. This one morning the water was up. It had rained all the night before, so the water was really rushing down the creek and under the foot log. Well, Barbara was afraid to go across. Everyone else was on the other side waiting for her. She was just standing there crying and would not even try to come across. We told her we would be late for school if she didn't come on; we even threatened to go on and leave her on the other side, but that didn't work. I also knew if we left her that I would get in trouble. So I went back across and took her by the hand, finally got her started walking across. She was still scared and crying. We got about half way across and she let go of my hand and refused to move; so I just went on and left her standing there looking at the rushing water under the log. I yelled at her to come on or she would fall in. I guess that got her attention; she came on across. From then on she walked the log; but she never was any good at it.

A little ways from the creek, if you went along the right side, there was a small log house where some people by the name of Moler lived part of the time. They usually left in the winter when the water flowed over their fields and around the little house. They had put some beehives down by the woods at the edge of their field. Well, of course us kids knew about the beehives. When it turned real cold, the water all around the little house and beehives froze over. One morning on our way to school we decided to skate through that way and go see the bees. Of course the bees weren't doing anything; they were too cold. So we had the idea that in the evening on our way home we would skate by the beehives and get us some honeycomb to eat. Well, the sun had shined all that day and by the time we started skating by the beehives there was water on top of the ice. The sun had melted the top of the ice and the bees were swarming all over the place; the sun had warmed them up, too. As we skated by they got mad and started flying after us. Bub and our cousin James ran up anyway and grabbed a handful of the honeycomb. But as we all took off running across the ice to escape the bees, my little sister Joyce fell down. By the time we got back on the path where it was dry, she had wet feet.

In those days us girls all wore long cotton socks held up by elastic bands up over our knees. Well, Joyce was crying; her feet were wet and cold. Bub and James had some matches so we decided to build a fire right there in the path. We told Joyce to take off her wet socks and we proceeded to hold them up over the fire to dry. My friend Dorothy was doing the holding; evidently she wasn't watching the proceedings very well. The socks got dry all right; they got so dry, one of them caught on fire and by the time we put the fire out, the whole foot of the sock was gone. We put the socks back on my little sister anyway and told her not to tell anyone about the bees or the socks or we would all get in trouble since we weren't supposed to go by the beehives or even go through the Molers' field or woods.

Beehives and Burned Socks

I don't know where Joyce put her socks that night, but the next day when we got home from school we were in big trouble: Aunt Tildie had found the socks with the foot burned out. It didn't take a genius to figure out what had happened. We all got a good tongue lashing for that, especially me, and Bub and James for having the matches, and me again for letting them build the fire. Socks weren't that easy to come by in those days either.

My baby brother Don, age 1; my baby sister Noma Lou, age 3, 1948

My cousins Billy Wayne and George Mack Clark, ages 2 and 4

- 15 -

Ground-puppies, Toad Frogs, Warts and Witches

My Uncle Wade and Aunt Imogene Clark and their kids George Mack and Billy Wayne moved over to a little place across from Grandma and Orville's farm when I was about ten or eleven and Bub was eight or nine. Aunt Imogene is Daddy's sister. The boys would come over to our place a lot. George was probably seven and Billy Wayne was about five. Daddy and Uncle Wade would go fishing a lot together. They would set out trotlines across the Cache River and catch big ole catfish to sell to other people. Daddy would get us kids to catch bait for them to put on the trotlines; we would catch spring frogs and dig big worms, or turn over an old rotting log and find grub-worms, toad frogs and ground-puppies. We kept the toad frogs to play with. We raced them or fed them flies.

We would chase George Mack with the ground-puppies; sometimes we called them water dogs (really they were salamanders). George was really afraid of them. We would chase him with the ground-puppies and bark at him, pretending it was the ground-puppies that were barking.

Daddy's youngest brother, Uncle Junior, had told all of us kids once that we shouldn't play with the water dogs, because, if they got mad and barked at you, you would die. Well none of us believed him (we knew the ground-puppies didn't bark) except George Mack; he believed Uncle Junior, so thereafter we gave him a hard time about the ground-puppies.

Also we were told we shouldn't play with the toad frogs, because if you accidentally killed one, the cows would give bloody milk; also if the toad peed on you, you would get warts. These sayings came to us from Grandma (Martin) Summers. We really didn't pay any attention to them; we just kept on playing with the toad frogs, but we were careful not to step on them or kill them.

We really did get warts, though. I had a big one on my wrist, and Betty had several appear on her legs and knees. She would fall down and make the one on her knee bleed. One day we were at Grandma's house and Betty had fallen down and hurt the wart on her knee, so Grandma told us to take some straws out of her broom and bring them to her. She took a broom straw and measured the wart on Betty's legs and knees, also the one on my wrist. She cut the straw the same size as the wart then took the pieces of straw and tied them in her handkerchief and put the handkerchief in her pocket. We then tried to get her to tell us what she was going to do with them. She just told us to go on outside and play and to forget about the straws and not to think about the warts either. You know that is exactly what we did, too. Even Betty didn't think about the one that was hurting on her knee.

A few weeks later we were at Grandma's house again. We had taken buckets of corn up to her place to grind into chops for our baby chickens, as we didn't have a corn grinder of our own. Well, we were busy grinding the corn when Grandma came out on the porch and started talking to us about the chops and our little chickens; then she asked us about our warts. We both looked for the warts at the same time. No warts were found anywhere. We never did find out why the warts went away; if she really made it happen or if it was just mind over matter. Maybe it was a little of both.

We always thought there was something a little strange about Grandma. She always had black curly hair that came from the beauty shop at Paragould and real dark eyes that could look right through a person. And when she was mad, you'd swear there was lightning flashing from them. It seemed like she was always mad at Orville, for some reason we never understood then. Later when we got older we found out: it was because she was so jealous-hearted. Mama said, "She has the eyes of the green-eyed monster." But us kids thought it was because she was a witch.

Ground-puppies, Toad Frogs, Warts and Witches

Grandma kept her hair cut real short and dyed black with a very curly perm in it. Orville called her Lula Belle. I never heard him call her by her real name, which was, Mammie Evelina (Battenfield) (Martin) Summers. It was no wonder he just called her Lula Belle, right? Really, he did it because of a cartoon lady he thought she looked like, and because it made her angry. Both of them just loved to fuss and argue. I know she wasn't really a witch, or she would have turned Orville into a toad frog.

Coffee Grounds and Grapevines

SWAMP FOG

Wet, raggedy clouds; come creeping,
Whimpering, shivering in the cold light
From a pale wintery sun.
Rags of mist. Beggars clothes.
Dogs wet hair: Shaking.
Trees; bare limbs sticking through fog.
Ghost shrouds; pleading – go away.
Fog; thick, gray, cold,
Here to stay.
Swamp water; muddy, dark, fog rising.
Smelly things old.
Telling stories from times untold.
Cypress knees, lungs of trees;
Reaching up in prayer form,
Searching for light.
Never knowing if – it's day or night.

—Eufa Eubanks-Adkison

Down by the creek that ran out from the old slough, wild grapevines grew, and all around the slough grew big old cypress trees, and all around the cypress trees grew their knees in all shapes and sizes. (Cypress knees are the roots of the cypress tree that grow up out of the ground and water so the tree can breathe.) Us kids would use that place for a playground in the summer when the old slough had dried up or in the winter when the water all around them froze real thick and hard. We would go there to skate. In the spring we went there and walked across the old trees that had fallen down and fished around the cypress knees. There were lots of perch and catfish to catch.

In the fall before the rains came and flooded it, we went there to play. We would swipe some of Daddy's cigarette papers and some coffee-grounds and matches and go sit around on the cypress knees and smoke the coffee grounds. When we couldn't get Daddy's cigarette papers, we used pieces of brown grocery bags for the cigarettes and sometimes we would smoke the grapevines in them. We would break the dead vines the length of cigarettes and light one end. You could smoke it because grapevines are hollow and have pith in them, kind of like the filters that real cigarettes have now.

When we smoked the wild grapevines we pretended we were Indians smoking peace pipes. Of course none of those things contained nicotine; what else they might have contained, I have no idea.

One fall it had rained a lot and the old slough had flowed all out in the woods; it stayed that way all winter. It was a very cold January that year. I was probably twelve or thirteen. One day it was really cold and snowing but Bub and I decided to go skating on the old slough; we skated around the cypress knees, then on around where the creek was and that was where the water was the deepest. Some of the old cypress logs had been floating in that deep water but had frozen. I started skating out toward the deep water and the ice started cracking. I couldn't stop and turn around because it was cracking behind me too. Bub had stopped and was yelling at me, "Hurry, hurry, get to the bank." I was trying but I went through the ice anyway in water that went right up to my armpits. I grabbed onto one of the cypress logs and hauled my wet dripping body onto the log. I jumped as far as I could. Being all wet, my coat, clothes and shoes were full of ice water but the log was close enough to the bank and the ice was thicker on the side next to the bank. I scrambled out onto the ground. By that time my brother was there and helped me up. I was freezing cold and turning blue. We took off as fast as we could go to the house. Mama was scared when she saw me. She started yelling, "Get those clothes off; get by the stove," like she had to tell me that!

You know, I didn't even get the sniffles over that. We didn't go skating down there again that winter. I thought about almost drowning and wondered if the devil was trying to get us for smoking the coffee-grounds and grapevines. I haven't decided that even after almost sixty years. You see Mama was always telling us when something bad happened to us it was the devil trying to get us for doing something we weren't supposed to do.

Brownie School, 1946

First Row, left to right:
Joyce Sullivan, Jessie Lyons, Floyd Clayton, Peggy Anderson, Joyce Eubanks, Denise Odem, Bea White, Doris Asher, Jacky Asher, Johnny Lyons.

Second Row:
Betty Eubanks, Floella Jackson, James Sullivan, James Pitcher, Billy Joe Newman, Leland White, Alvin (Bub) Eubanks, Wayne Lyons, George Mack Clark.

Third Row:
Eufa Eubanks, Rosalee Asher, Brenda Newman, Jeneva Asher, Jenetta Asher, Mrs. Vesta Varvell (Teacher), Charlene Scott, Dorothy Van Pool, Lorene Sullivan, Shirley Osburn.

I hope I got everyone's name right; it's been more than fifty years! I was thirteen in this photo. Some of the kids weren't there that day: my little sister Alma and my cousin Barbara, and a few others I can't think of.

- 17 -

Sex, Rabbits, and Violence

Ms. Vesta Varvill was the teacher at Brownie School, the one-room school in the country. She taught all us kids from grades one through eight. To me, she was the best teacher in the world. She let us have a baseball team. Both girls and boys played on the same team, because there weren't enough of either to make a team.

Since we had no bus, she would arrange for transportation so we could go to the other schools to play them, schools like Peach Orchard and Delaplaine. When I was eleven, twelve and thirteen, I lived to go to school to play ball. My brother and I considered ourselves to be the best players on the team; all the other kids on the team seemed to think that way too. We had gotten to be the big shots at school by that time.

When I was twelve and Bub was ten, some people by the name of Lyons bought the house on the corner across from the school. They put in a grocery store in the front room of the house. They had three boys: Wayne, Jessie and Johnny. Wayne was the oldest, about my age, and from the time he started to go to school with us, he considered himself my boyfriend. There was a girl by the name of Shirley Osburn going to school with us. She was Bub's age and considered by everyone to be his girlfriend.

Ms. Vesta took advantage of these facts (if they were facts). Just before Valentine's Day, she decided that the school would put on a play. I don't know where she got the script. The play was called "The Heavenly Twins." Guess who got the leading roles? Shirley, Bub, Wayne, and I. Shirley and I were the girl twins and Bub and Wayne the boy twins. The girls' parents decided to send the girls off to a private girls school. The boys didn't like that at all, so they would dress up as girls and sneak into the girls' school.

Close to the end of the play the boys had to kiss the girls. It took a lot of coaxing from Ms. Vesta to finally get that accomplished. There was a lot of laughing and giggling and whispering going on from the other kids. Ms. Vesta had a lot of courage and patience. She finally got us ready to put on the play.

On the day of the play, Wayne and Shirley got permission from their parents to go home with Bub and I, presumably to study the play, as our parts had about ten or twelve pages of script to memorize.

We already knew all of the play; they just wanted to go to our house.

Daddy had said he would take us that night; so all the family and the two friends loaded into our old steel-tired wagon and headed out through the woods at night in the middle of February to the old one-room schoolhouse, which was all set up for the play. All the parents were supposed to come watch us put on the play.

All of us kids were in the back of the old wagon jolting along covered up with quilts. About half way to the school, Wayne got up and went to sit on the wagon seat behind my dad, and in a voice that could be heard for miles, (or so I thought), he exclaimed, "Mr. Eubanks, when I grow up I'm going to marry Eufa!" Well, I just wanted to jump out of that wagon and run away out into the woods and hide. (Good-grief! Didn't he know you didn't say that kind of thing to my dad?) But to my surprise, my dad just laughed and said, "OK." That made me feel even worse. I didn't think I could ever get through that play in front of my parents now. But when we got to the school and I saw Ms. Vesta and the great expectation in her eyes, I knew I had to do it for her. I just kept saying to myself, "This is not real, this is only a dream," or maybe a nightmare. When the play was over, everyone thought it was great. Ms. Vesta said she was real proud of us. I wasn't used to getting praise for anything.

I know now that Ms. Vesta was just teaching us self-confidence, something we surely would need a lot of later. I guess also that night and that play taught me my first lesson in sex education.

However, the gross part of sex education I learned from going rabbit hunting with my brother and cousins.

We went out into the woods, which were all around our place, to go hunting. We found a rabbit and tried to sneak up close enough to hit it with a stick or shoot it with a slingshot (most of the times we missed). But the rabbit ran off through the woods with us kids chasing after it. We chased it until it got tired; so it found an old hollow log and ran into it. But all was not lost. We got a long limb off a bush and proceeded to get the rabbit out of the log by twisting the limb up into its fur and then yanking on it. Finally by doing that many times, we pulled it out; when we did there wasn't any fur left on that poor rabbit except on its head and in the last bit we had the limb twisted up. The poor thing was squeaking and carrying on something awful so my brother hit it on the head with a big stick and killed it. Then we decided to cook it; so we built a bonfire, hung the rabbit up on a limb and started to dress it out. Guess what? It wasn't a "he." It was a "she." And she was going to have babies; they were there inside and were still alive.

I don't know why, but after what we did to that rabbit, and seeing the baby rabbits and not knowing what to do or think, we got scared and ashamed. We went back a little later on and of course the babies were dead; we took the rabbit and her babies and buried them and went home.

Some of the younger kids had been with us; one of them told Mama (I think it was Joyce) about the baby rabbits. Joyce thought the mother rabbit had eaten the babies. Mama knew better, of course. She didn't like what Joyce was telling her we did, so we got a good preaching to.

I asked Mama why the baby rabbits were inside the mother rabbit and how they got there if she didn't eat them. The answer I got was, "That's just the way rabbits are; now get out of here before I give you a whipping." So much for my sex education. We did learn we weren't to kill animals in such a violent manner and just for what we thought at the time was fun.

I think when I was that age, if someone had said, "will the real Huckleberry Finn stand up," I would have had to stand up.

Wayne Lyons,
1947

Cousin Barbara

Me (Eufa) with my friend
Regina Reynolds; we were
thirteen

Aunt Tildie doing laundry
while I take care
of Noma Lou, 1946

- 18 -

The Watermelon

When I was about fourteen, some people moved into an old house about halfway between our place and the one-room school we went to. It was on the road to Brownie School.

Their names were the Van Pooles. There were four kids in the family at that time; the two oldest were girls. Dorothy was my age; Vata May was my sister Betty's age. Of course we got to know them because they had to go to Brownie School with us.

This would be in July and August. That's when we went to school, before the cotton was ready to be picked. It is really hot in the bottomlands in northeastern Arkansas in the middle of summer; two miles got to be a long hot walk, especially in your bare feet. We never wore shoes in the summer—probably because we didn't have any.

The Van Poole kids were in the same financial situation as us kids, probably even worse. I think their dad sharecropped for some other man.

Well, on this day in mid-August we were all walking home from school. Dorothy and I got ahead of the younger kids and I made a suggestion. Dorothy had asked if she could go home with me to do homework. Her Mama said OK. Now the other kids had gotten ahead of us, so we let them go on ahead toward my house, because we had another idea.

In between our place and theirs was Molers' cornfield, down beside which was their watermelon patch. The cornfield was quite large and so were the cornstalks. We walked in the corn patch between the rows; it was shaded by the cornstalks so it was a lot cooler on bare feet in the shade. When we got to the very last row, there was the watermelon patch. Huge melons were lying there—we could just pull one off the vine and roll it into the corn patch. If we lay down on our stomachs no one would see us. So down we went onto the scorching hot ground, pulled a huge melon into the cornrow middles and pushed it in front of us while we crawled far enough into the corn patch so Mr. Moler or the other kids wouldn't see us. We then stood up; I got one end of the melon and Dorothy took the other end; we raised it up then let go—it broke into several pieces there on the hot dusty ground. We ate that boiling hot melon, dirt and all. While we were eating, talking and giggling, Vata May and Betty snuck into the corn patch from the other side and found us, and of course, told on us. By the time we got to my house we were sick; we ran back down into the woods and chucked up the watermelon all over the place.

Then Mama told us we had to see Mr. Moler and tell him what we did and ask him how much he wanted for the watermelon. He said he would talk to my dad about it. So he did. It so happened that we had stolen his prized watermelon.

The first money we made that fall from picking cotton for Uncle Isaac went to pay Mr. Moler for his melon, instead of for a pair of shoes.

Neither one of us wanted to eat any more watermelon for a long time. I don't know about Dorothy, but that was the first time I ever stole anything.

To this very day when I eat watermelon, I think of that very hot day and a girlfriend named Dorothy.

Grandpa Eubanks

I guess my Grandpa Eubanks was the most educated person in our family when I was a kid. I know he farmed; he would have had to. He and Grandma Martha had ten kids. My daddy was their third child; there were seven boys and three girls.

He farmed to make a living for them.

I never remember seeing Grandpa with a pair of overalls on, though.

All the other men I knew who farmed, wore old blue overalls and brown work shirts.

I wasn't around Grandpa very much. It seems like he was gone off someplace a lot. By the time I was old enough to remember much, all my uncles and aunts were grown except for Uncle Duane and Uncle Junior, who were the babies of the family. They were around seven and nine years older than me. One time I remember Bub and I went home with Grandma Eubanks to stay the night. The next day we were playing out around their old barn. Junior and Duane climbed up on the roof of the barn; Bub and I started throwing corncobs and horse turds at them; they just laughed at us and started peeing on our heads. Of course we went in and told Grandma. The uncles got in trouble. They were quite ornery and were always getting in trouble with Grandma; she had an Irish temper.

Grandma Eubanks passed away when I was twelve. She had a heart condition. I think she was either fifty-seven or fifty-eight when she died.

The uncles were still at home; they were teenagers then, probably seventeen and nineteen years old. Grandpa was away someplace when Grandma passed away. Someone said he was down on Black River fishing.

After Grandma died, Grandpa and the boys moved to Delaplaine. Grandpa wasn't farming any more. I don't know if that was the years he worked for the Cache River Drainage Association or not. I know he worked for them and was the Justice of the Peace at Delaplaine.

I remember him marrying people. He had a lot of law books in his house where he lived across the railroad tracks at Delaplaine, the same side the cotton gin was on. But one night his house caught fire and burned up all of his law books and most everything he owned.

Duane joined the Army. I don't remember what Junior did at that time; he lived with Aunt Imogene, I think.

Grandpa moved into the big old house that used to be the hotel at Delaplaine. He lived there when I got married and after my husband came back from Korea, we lived in part of that big old house with Grandpa; it was where I lived when my first daughter was born.

Grandpa Eubanks lived to be eighty-six, I think. I remember him best, there in that big old hotel house at Delaplaine, sitting in his rocking chair by the old potbellied wood heating stove with his pipe in his mouth, wearing khaki pants and a cardigan sweater; looking very much the old English squire.

My grandpa, Mack Eubanks.
This picture was taken about 1956
in the old hotel house at Delaplaine, Arkansas.

- 20 -

Chocolate Pudding and Blackbird Dumplin's

There were two more sisters and a brother born after we moved to the thirty-seven acres over by Uncle Isaac and Aunt Jessie's place on Cache River, or as everyone called it, Kinfolks Island. The first one born there was my sister Alma Fay. She had black hair and brown eyes that sparkled and everyone thought she was real cute. I thought she was just another kid I would have to help take care of, which was true; but I also knew that when she got big enough she would have to chop and pick cotton, which was also true.

It was four years before Mama had another baby, also another girl. I was twelve years old then.

This sister was named Noma Lou, and she was "puny a lot," Mama's words, not my opinion. Mama had a hard time having this baby. Aunt Tildie had gone off some place to work for someone at the time that Noma Lou was born, so Daddy and us other kids did the housework and took care of Mama. Daddy would do most of the cooking, and in those days after a baby was born the mother would have to stay in bed for nine days in order to get well. That's what the doctors and midwives thought they should do, so that's what Mama did. Usually Aunt Tildie was there to do the laundry and the cooking, with our help, but not this time.

Anyway, while Mama was recuperating, Daddy decided to make us some chocolate pudding. Then it didn't come in a box; you had to make it from scratch—cocoa, sugar, flour, milk and vanilla. Daddy got all the ingredients together, cooked it on the old wood-burning cook stove, then he put it in a big old crock bowl Mama had used for years. He then decided to put meringue on the top of the pudding. He beat egg whites and sugar together, made a real nice meringue, put it in the oven to brown, all us kids were watching, anxious to eat it. He took it out of the oven and was really pleased. He wanted to show his masterpiece to Mama so across the kitchen he went with the bowl of pudding, holding it out in front of him. He got to the bedroom door (which was also the living room) and ka-plop, the whole bottom of the old crock bowl fell out, chocolate pudding went flying all over the floor.

Us kids giggled; that was the wrong thing to do!

Daddy walked calmly to the spoon holder, gave each kid a spoon and looked down at the chocolate mess on the floor and quietly said, "Eat!" Alma was four years old at the time; I think she ate more pudding and got more on herself than anyone else. Thereafter she was called Alma Fudge instead of Alma Fay.

This was in April and the blackbirds were coming through our fields real bad that spring; there would be great black clouds of them. They were getting on Daddy's nerves I guess, so he got his old shotgun and some birdshot and Ka-boom. I think he must have got a couple of dozen of them and us kids helped him skin the feathers off them. He took those old blackbirds and put them in a pot, boiled them and made dumplings. Or as we called them, "dumplin's."

That is the first and the last time I remember eating blackbird dumplin's. I'm sure I would remember if I'd had them again.

Mr. Bill, Mrs. Bessie, Leland, and Bea

Right across the road from the one-room Brownie school there was a little old log house. Mr. Bill White lived there with his wife, Mrs. Bessie, their son, Leland, and their daughter, little Beatrice Marie (everyone just called her Bea).

Mr. Bill was the janitor for the school. In the wintertime he would go build a fire in the big old wood-burning stove in the schoolhouse and sweep the floor, stuff like that. He was a little fat man; Mrs. Bessie was a little lady and almost blind. Us kids thought of them as being old, but I'm sure they weren't, or they wouldn't have had kids that age, as Leland was about my brother Bub's age, and Bea was about three when we first started going to school there. My brother was five and I was seven. Our cousin Esther was fourteen; we walked to school and back with her.

Esther was real finicky. She would make me and Bub carry her lunch and if we had to wear boots, on account of the water and mud, we had to carry her shoes too. If we wouldn't carry her lunch, she threw it in the woods, and come lunchtime she would make us give part of ours to her. I guess you would say she was a bully, huh?

The first year we went to school at Brownie, Mr. Emil Thomas was the teacher.

I guess Mrs. Bessie had a hard time watching after Bea, because sometimes she would come over to the school and just walk in and start playing around. Sometimes she didn't wear many clothes. One day she came and didn't have on any underwear; all she had on was a little old dirty dress. She wasn't there but a few minutes until she went wee-wee on the floor.... Mr. Emil had Leland take her home. Leland was very embarrassed, because of course everyone laughed at Bea.

During Christmas time that year we had a Christmas play and program. Everyone was to bring a present for their kids to open, and Santa Claus (Mr. Bill) would give out candy; otherwise most of us kids wouldn't even get any.

My dad, Uncle Isaac, and my Step-grandpa Orville decided to give Mr. Bill a Christmas present; but they were just being mischievous. They got a big turnip and wrapped it in a bunch of pages from a Montgomery Ward catalog; then they put it in a cardboard box and then put that box into a larger box; finally they had four boxes in all, the last one being quite large. Aunt Tildie had some red crepe paper. So they had her wrap the box with that and make a big bow also out of the crepe paper; it made a real Christmas-looking package. They put Mr. Bill's name on it. So that night at the program they put the package under the Christmas tree. When Santa (Mr. Bill) saw his package, he was real pleased that someone had given him a present. Daddy, Uncle Isaac and Orville were anxious for him to open it so they could have a big laugh on him.

Mr. Bill started opening all the boxes; everyone was watching. He finally came to the turnip—when he saw what it was, he just smiled and said "Thank you, this will make a good Christmas lunch tomorrow." The guys weren't so pleased with their joke then, because they knew Mr. Bill really did like his present.

You see they weren't going to have much of a Christmas dinner at his house. Daddy said he would never try playing a joke on Mr. Bill again. I'm glad they never did what I heard them talking about giving him: horse biscuits, which would have really been a mean thing to do.

- 22 -

The Raft

It seemed like someone was always moving in and out of the little old log house over by the Molers' farm.

When I was twelve or thirteen some people moved into it; their name was Reynolds. I think they came from up north, somewhere around St. Louis. They had two girls: one was my age, her name was Regina, my dad nicknamed her Shanklegs. Her sister, Joanna, was my sister Betty's age.

They started going to school at Brownie with us kids and would come to our house a lot to play and go to church with us. It seemed like their mom and dad were never home. I don't know what they did for a living; worked for one of the other farmers, I guess.

It seemed like they didn't care much where the girls were. I don't think Mr. Reynolds was their real dad (of course that's how it seemed to me, being a kid). They were treated differently by him than we were treated by our dad. Anyway, the girls would rather be at our house.

They liked going to church with us. Joanna could sing real nice and wasn't a bit bashful; she would get up in front of everyone and sing the gospel song, "In the Garden." Everyone at church liked to hear her sing; sometimes Regina would sing with her.

They didn't like to work very much though. Daddy tried to get them to pick cotton for him, but that didn't go over too well. They didn't think kids were supposed to work like that, especially little girls; they said their mom didn't think so either.

Daddy didn't appreciate their views of course, but he never told them they couldn't come to our house. They just knew we had to work in the fields so they didn't come when we were picking or chopping cotton.

Right behind our chicken house was where the old slough started. When it rained the water was quite deep and came right up behind the chicken house. That way we never had to pump and carry water for the chickens; *but*...there was a drawback to that, especially for the baby chicks and when we once tried to raise some baby ducks. You see, the snapping turtles and water moccasins had claimed that old slough as their home for many years before the chickens and ducks and kids had come on the scene. So it's no wonder fowl was number one on their menu.

The only thing that kept us kids from being the second course was that we knew how to keep away from the turtles and water moccasins...I think.

One spring morning, Regina and Joanna came over for a visit. We all went out to play. What could we do on a beautiful June day? (It had rained the night before so we didn't have to chop cotton. It was too muddy.)

Regina and I decided to build a raft; all the other kids were in for the idea, so we all got busy and cut down a bunch of willow bushes. (Oh, yes, we knew how to cut bushes with chopping axes, as we had gotten a lot of practice clearing the thirty-seven acre farm.)

We got all our poles made and cut strips of bark from some of the poles in order to tie the poles together. We had quite a raft made by the middle of the afternoon. We made two poles with which to push the raft. Everyone wanted to go for a ride. But we couldn't do that, because it would sink with so many kids on it. So Regina and I decided to try it out first as we were the oldest; then we would take two of the younger kids at a time for a ride. Nice plan, huh?

Well, we pushed off; the water was deep. Our push-poles were almost not long enough. We got out to about the middle of the slough. Here comes a big ol' water moccasin swimming toward us. The other kids were yelling to us about it. We tried to turn the raft around to go back to the bank, but our push-poles wouldn't reach the bottom, so we tried to paddle with them. All of a sudden, the raft started coming apart.

    The willow bark was wet and slick and came untied. As the raft came all apart, we fell into the water with the water moccasin. The other kids started throwing sticks and stuff at it. Regina and I were treading water as fast as we could. Finally, our feet touched the muddy bottom, which stirred up the snapping turtles; but we were splashing and screaming so much it must have scared the snap outta them; we didn't get bit or snapped, but we sure enough were scared and wet and muddy when we got out of that old slough. We took off up to where our pump was and pumped water on each other until we got clean. We went and sat in the sunshine until we got dry. We decided to let the turtles and snakes have the old slough.

    For that day, anyhow.

Us kids in the cotton wagon. This was in 1949; we were coming up in the world, had a new wagon with rubber tires!

A family reunion about 1947, everyone standing in a cotton patch by our house on the thirty-seven acre farm.

- 23 -

The Quicksand Hole

Up the road toward Peach Orchard, about a mile from the one-room school, there was a farm. It was a large farm, compared to our thirty-seven acres. It had a big house and several out-buildings.

It was owned by people named the Ashers. They were a large family; some of the kids went to school with us. There were twin girls a little older than me. Their names were Geneva and Gennetta. There was another girl named Rosalee, a boy named Jacky, and another boy that was older than the twins. His name was Wilbert; he was my cousin Esther's age.

There were older kids than him, but they were out of school and I've since forgotten their names.

Anyway, Wilbert and Esther started liking each other when they were still going to school and got to be girl and boy friends when they were sixteen and seventeen. I guess that was the last year they went to school.

One night there was a pie supper at the schoolhouse. I didn't know what it was for, but all the girls had to bake a pie to take. The boys were supposed to buy a pie and whoever got a certain girl's pie had to eat it with that girl. Aunt Tildie made two pies: one for herself and one for me to take.

Wilbert came over to pick up Esther, Aunt Tildie, me, my brother Bub, my sister Betty, and, of course, Barbara, my cousin, Esther's little sister. We all got into the wagon. It was almost dark when we got started through the woods on the way to the schoolhouse. Wilbert decided to take a shortcut; he said he knew of one. After we finally got started my brother and I both told him it wasn't a good idea to go that way. We knew those woods better than he did, as we played around all over them and had been walking through them to school for three or four years; but of course he didn't listen to us because he thought he was grown up and knew everything and we were just little ole snotty-nose kids. But before that night was over he thought about listening to us some from then on.

But you know how the saying goes: "A lesson earned is a lesson learned."

Anyway, that night we got about a quarter of a mile from our house and all of a sudden we stopped. The team of horses was up to their knees in a quicksand hole and the wagon was buried up to the front axles of the wheels. The horses couldn't pull the wagon out, so there we set. Wilbert got out onto the tongue of the wagon and unfastened the horses from it and told them to move. And they did, right straight out of that quicksand and right out through the woods back to Uncle Isaac's barnyard, leaving the wagon behind.

Wilbert got out the back end of the wagon past the quicksand. He helped Esther and Aunt Tildie get out; then he carried us kids out on his back, one at a time. We had to walk back to our house through the dark woods.

Wilbert and Uncle Isaac went the next morning and pulled the wagon out backwards from the quicksand hole.

About a year later, Esther and Wilbert got married. Then Wilbert had to go into the Army as the war was still going on in Japan and Germany.

He was gone a long time. While he was gone, Esther had a little baby boy; she named him Henry Lee. Wilbert made it back from the war all right and was a lot more grown up than the night of the quicksand hole.

- 24 -

The Missing Tractor

*An old mule will live to be a hundred years old
waiting around to get a chance just to get
to kick your head off.*

Those were my daddy's sentiments about the last two ole mules he owned. Their names were Old Red and Old Jim (nice unimaginative names, huh?) Well! That was the only thing unimaginative about them! They were as ornery as old mules come. If they wanted to go someplace, fences didn't matter to them. If the fences were too high for them to jump over they just tore them down, tromped them and walked right over them.

I sure didn't like those two ole mules and I was afraid of them. My brother Bub and I would have to go find them when they got out. They would go hide in the woods and if they saw us they would run and hide somewhere else. When we finally got them home and in the barn lot, we had to go fix the fences they had torn down. Once after we had gotten them in the barn lot and left them to go fix the fence, when we got back we found out that they had killed a calf. Our old milk cow and her calf were in the barn lot also. I guess those ole mules were mad because we had made them go in the barn lot so they took it out on that poor little calf. So you can see why I was afraid of them!

This was about the year I turned eighteen and Bub was sixteen. He sure did hate those old mules too. He would shoot them with his BB gun; but they were so mean and tough the BB's just bounced off their hides.

I guess that year Daddy must have made some extra money off the cotton crop, because he bought a tractor.

I remember the day he bought it. Dad, Uncle Isaac and Orville went to an International Harvester show at Pocahontas, Arkansas. My friend Laura (the preacher's daughter) and I went to the tractor show with them. That must have been the spring of 1951. Daddy and Uncle Isaac both bought a tractor; I was really glad. Now Daddy could get rid of those old mean mules. They were so mean and tough, the mosquitoes could only bite them on the nose and ears; then only if they could catch them.

After Daddy brought the tractor home he worked from daylight until after dark in the fields. About three days after he brought the tractor home, he was up by daylight that morning and went out to start it, but it was gone. No sign of it anywhere, not even any tracks.

Daddy came back in the house and told Mama the tractor was gone. Then he started off looking for it or for a sign of what might have happened to it. He walked down toward the old drainage ditch (Cache River). There was an old slough back there too. Lo and behold—there set the nice new red International Tractor—and around it lay five huge swampland mosquitoes with their bills and legs sticking straight up in the air deader than a door knob, and full of gas and oil too! You see they thought that nice red tractor was an ole mule, and they flew off with it to the slough to feast in peace, as it didn't give any resistance. (I know what you are thinking.)

But you don't know how big swampland mosquitoes were back then! —You also know this last part is a big lie, don't you? Mosquitoes hate the smell of gas!

This is just a story my dad would tell people in town when they would start talking about how big the mosquitoes were that particular year.

Eufa and the tractor

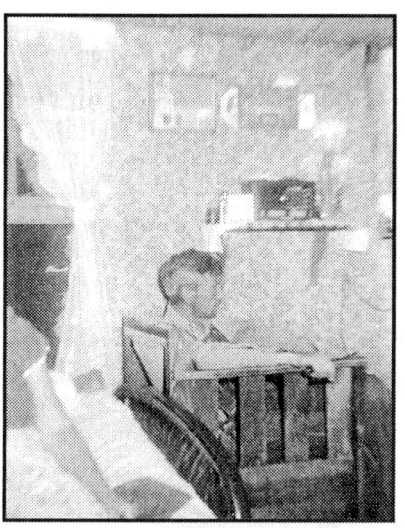

Daddy, in 1955, in the living room of our old house after we got electricity. Mama was sitting on the bed; this was also their bedroom.

Family photo, everyone except Betty and Aunt Tildie

World War II

In 1941, I was eight years old. I can remember all the grownups talking about "how there was going to be a war."

I could tell by the things I heard them say, that war was not a good thing. I really didn't know what it was or what it would have to do with us.

But a few months later, in December to be exact, I knew a lot more about it. On December the seventh we got to school and the teacher told us that some people called "the Japanese" had dropped something called "bombs" on a place somewhere called "Pearl Harbor" and the bombs killed a lot of Americans. I remember being very scared, because for all I knew, that place could be right down the road, somewhere close by.

When we got home from school, Daddy was listening to the radio. It was some man telling us about the awful things that had happened at that place called Pearl Harbor and I knew it was this thing called "a war." Then I heard Mama and Aunt Tildie talking. Mama said they were making all the able-bodied men go fight those Japanese, and that Daddy might have to go help. That just about scared me to death. I didn't want my dad to go fight anyone, anywhere.

For the next several days and nights that's all I could think about because I didn't understand why people were fighting and killing each other and why someone called "the President" would want my daddy to go there. I sure didn't want anyone to hurt him. I wondered what in the world that war had to do with us, anyway.

In the next four years I sure found out what war meant and what it had to do with an eight-year-old on a little ole farm in the back of nowhere, Arkansas. I had nightmares all that year. I would dream about those bombs exploding in the sky over our house and dream that those Japanese and Germans were coming through our yard and into our house and that they had guns and were shooting at each other.

Finally, I understood Daddy wasn't going to have to go to the war and that the war was in a place called Japan and Germany and that was a long way across a lot of water. So I figured the bad people couldn't come to our house and Daddy wasn't going over there. So things got a little better...in my dreams, anyway.

I remember the first airplane I ever saw. It flew over our cotton patch. That was also very scary. We stood and watched it until it was out of sight. I learned later the airplanes were going to the airbase down by Little Rock. But then I didn't even know where Little Rock was, or that it was the capital of Arkansas.

The teacher would talk about all those things at school; so it wasn't long before I figured out a lot of stuff. Mostly she was talking to the older kids, but it was a one-room school. I would listen to her talking to the big kids instead of doing the schoolwork I was supposed to be doing.

Remember, there wasn't television in those days. All we had were radios and if you didn't understand what people were talking about in the news, there were no pictures to show you what it was they were saying. You just used your imagination, and listened to the teacher at school, and asked her questions if you were brave enough.

I remember there were a lot of things we couldn't get because of the war, even if you had the money to buy those things (which we mostly didn't), like tires and sugar and shoes. They were rationed. You got a book of stamps called ration books. You got a certain amount of stamps for each thing that was rationed. Each person in the household got their own amount, and it wasn't much.

I remember going around hunting for old broken iron things, like old plows, and rubber things, like old worn-out tires, and rubber boots that couldn't be patched anymore. We would take those things into town where they were picked up and sent to factories that were making weapons for war.

In the spring of 1945, I was almost twelve. The war had been going on for over four years.

On May 8, I got to school in the morning and some of the kids were already there. The teacher was telling them that the war was over in Germany; that Hitler had surrendered. The teacher let each of us kids ring the big bell, one time each, and to us that made the war final.

But it really wasn't, as Japan was still fighting our troops in the Pacific.

That is when President Harry Truman made the decision to drop the atomic bomb on Hiroshima, Japan, August 6, 1945. Then after three days another bomb was dropped on Nagasaki. After about a week, Japan surrendered.

World War II was a very bad war. But aren't they all?

I guess it seemed so bad to me because I was a kid, and that's when I learned what war meant.

After that war, some people were going around to all the small towns where there were cotton gins. They were showing us how to make mattresses out of cotton. Mama, Aunt Tildie, Aunt Jessie, Grandma and Aunt Mary all went out to Delaplaine to one of the mattress-making shows. They got to make us some mattresses for our beds, as all we had to sleep on were the straw mattresses or feather beds we had made from the ducks' feathers we had picked. The straw mattresses had to be redone each fall. We cut down a lot of dry grass and stuff (weeds, I suppose) and stuffed the mattress covers, which were made out of cotton flour or feed sacks.

We were real happy to get the cotton mattresses, even if there were no springs in them, just solid cotton batting stitched through in a lot of places with thread like twine.

That was my bed until I got married and bought a real factory-made mattress.

Joyce, Betty, Noma Lou and Alma, about 1950

Eufa and Laura Harlan going fishing, 1949

Betty and Joyce in their cotton picking clothes, 1949

Turtle Soup, Hominy, and Lye Soap

When I was six years old and my brother Bub was four, we were still living on the old German man's farm, where Daddy sharecropped.

In the winter months Daddy worked for the WPA, or Works Progress Administration, which was a New Deal work program. It was started by Franklin D. Roosevelt in 1935 and gave jobs to people so that the nation could get out of the Great Depression. The Great Depression was going on when I was born. And things weren't much better when I was six.

The school at Delaplaine was built by the WPA workers. By 1943, when it officially ended, around 8,500,000 people had worked for the WPA.

That winter of 1938-39, when Daddy worked for it, I remember he got paid around Christmas time and bought us kids oranges and apples and some candy for Christmas. I remember it being the best Christmas at that time of my life.

That spring, Bub and I went down to the river to fish. Cache River Drainage Ditch also ran right by the sharecrop farm. We would go through the barnyard and through the woods for a short distance and there was the ditch (or river). Anyway, it was a good place to fish. Aunt Tildie went with us as Mama wouldn't let us go by ourselves at that time.

On this day the fish were not biting at all, which made us get tired real quick. So we decided to set out our fishing poles and leave them there so that maybe a catfish would get on them during the night. It was raining the next morning so we couldn't go see if we had caught anything. That evening when Daddy came home he said he would go check our fishing poles for us. When he came back we saw him coming through the barn yard dragging something. We ran to meet him. He was dragging a HUGE loggerhead turtle. He had tied the fishing line around its front legs so he could drag it. Mama asked him why he had brought that thing into the house. He told her the turtle shell would make a good watering pan for the chickens, and that he was going to make soup out of the meat from the turtle. We wondered how he was going to cook that huge thing.

Daddy filled the big black wash kettle full of water and built a fire under it. He got a chopping ax, and when the turtle stuck his head out of his shell—*whack!* Dad chopped its head off. Then he chopped off its feet and tail. Then he got a big butcher knife and took off the bottom shell before taking out the entrails. He then picked up the rest of the turtle, top shell and all, and put it in the big wash-kettle. It would hardly fit. The shell was too big. Well! Daddy boiled that thing for hours. When he finally got the shell off, he took it out of the kettle; and cooked the turtle some more. But it was still too tough. You know, I can't remember if we ate any of that turtle or not. I think Daddy tried to, anyway

The turtle wasn't the only thing dad cooked in that wash kettle; he also made hominy. He would shell a big dishpan full of field corn and put it in the wash kettle with a lot of water. He would get ashes he had saved from the wood-burning heating stove and put them in a cloth, tie the cloth up real tight and put it in the kettle with the corn and water. He would then let it set until the next day, take out the ashes, build a fire under the wash kettle, and boil the corn until the husks were soft enough to come off the kernels of corn. Then he dipped out the corn, washed it until all the husk was off, put it back in the kettle with clean water and cooked it until the corn was soft. That was hominy. And it was good too, better than what you can buy in cans nowadays!

In the late fall, after the weather turned cold, we butchered hogs. Mama and Aunt Tildie would take all the fat off the intestines of the hogs, and some of the skin too, and put all that in the big wash kettle and cook it until nothing much was left except a lot of grease and cracklings from the skin. We

Turtle Soup, Hominy, and Lye Soap

kept part of the grease to cook with; it's called lard. The rest of the grease we used to make soap. We used the old wash-kettle to do that also.

To make soap, you first made some lye water from the ashes out of the wood heating stove. A few days before Mom was going to make soap, Daddy would burn only oak wood in the heating stove. Hardwood makes the best ashes for making lye water. Daddy would take the ashes out in the morning before he built a fire. He tied them up in a flour sack, like he did when he made hominy. He put the sacks of ashes in the old wash kettle and covered it with water then let it set for a day or two. He then took the bags of ashes out and there was lye water. Mama and Aunt Tildie would do the rest. They put some of the grease they had rendered from the hog fat into the lye water and it would start boiling and boil until the lye was neutralized by the fat. They would then stir it with a big wooden paddle while it was boiling (you had to be real careful not to let any splash on you or in your eyes). When it stopped boiling it looked like pudding or tan-colored Jello. When it cooled down, they dipped it out of the wash kettle and put it into dishpans to harden; this took another two or three days, I think. They then took it out of the dishpans, laid it on boards and cut it into bars. That was our laundry detergent and also our bath soap and shampoo. It got things really clean and sanitized. Do you believe it?

I remember watching my parents and aunts do these things from when I was around six until I was twelve or fourteen. One time I remember Mama and Aunt Tildie making lye soap and they used a can of store-bought lye instead of making it themselves. Aunt Tildie was pouring the can of lye into the water and boiling grease in the wash kettle when some of it splashed into her eye. This was when I was six years old, but I can still remember how she screamed and cried. Mama got hold of her and made her put her head underneath the pump spout. Then Mama pumped cold water into her face and eye until she calmed down. They put grease all over her face and around her eye and bandaged it up. We had no way to get her to the doctor since Daddy was working for the WPA at the time and had gone to work with the only transportation we had: a team of horses and an old steel-tired wagon.

Aunt Tildie's eye finally got well, but she didn't have as much sight in it as before. Several years after that, she had to get eyeglasses.

I remember how poor we were back then. I can still hear my daddy saying, "A poor person ain't got no more business out from under the ground than a mole."

My daddy passed away at the age of fifty; I always thought he had worked too hard.

Grandpa Martin

I don't remember seeing my Grandpa Martin (Mama's dad) when I was little. I was probably around nine or ten years old when I first remember him coming to visit us. He would come to Aunt Jessie's house mostly. He didn't seem like he wanted to be around a bunch of little kids much. They had ten kids, so maybe that is why he and Grandma got divorced. I've heard Mama say he wasn't around much when she was a kid either.

Grandpa Martin was a small man with piercing blue eyes and straight black hair. He was Cherokee Indian; Mama said he would just take off walking and not come home for months at a time. She didn't know where he went and neither did Grandma. He would come home for a little while and Grandma would have another baby to take care of and Grandpa would be off again someplace doing whatever it was he did.

I think Grandpa was born in Georgia and came to Oklahoma with his dad and mom when he was a young boy. He and Grandma were married in Blunt, Oklahoma, in 1906, while Oklahoma was still Indian Territory and a year before it became a state in 1907. That was the year their first child, Aunt Jessie, was born. My mama, Sadie, was the second child, born at Sallisaw, Oklahoma, in 1909.

Grandpa and Grandma were divorced in 1933 before I was born. That is when Aunt Tildie (one of Mama's younger sisters) came to live with Mama and Daddy. She was thirteen then and had no one to take care of her, as Grandma had gone off to live with Orville Summers. There were kids younger than Aunt Tildie: two of them lived with my Aunt Jessie and Uncle Isaac. They were Aunt Mary and Aunt Mammie. Two others, also girls, were Aunt Mildred and Aunt Lily. Aunt Lily was Mama's baby sister. They were with Grandpa part of the time, as he had gotten married again. He married an old maid schoolteacher, who had no kids, named Corrie. They lived in Missouri at the time. Sometimes the girls came to live with Grandma and Orville after they got the farm across from ours.

I started knowing the girls when I was eight or nine. Aunt Lily was probably fourteen then. I remember she could play the guitar and sing. I would go up to Grandma's house to visit, because I liked being with Aunt Lily. She would play the guitar and sing an old ballad, called "Thorn Rosa." It would scare me. But kids like to be scared, you know, in a good way. They think it's fun.

In 1949, when I was seventeen and out of school, I picked cotton as usual. So did Aunt Tildie. Aunt Tildie and I took our cotton picking money, bought a bus ticket and went to Rockford, Illinois. That was where my cousin Esther and her husband Wilbert Asher had gone to live, so that Wilbert could get a job in the factories.

Aunt Tildie and I thought we could get a job there too. So much for wishful thinking; we stayed up there for three months and didn't find a job. We then decided to go to Oklahoma, where my Aunt Lula lived (Mama and Aunt Tildie's sister.) But we didn't have enough money for a bus ticket. Aunt Tildie wrote to Grandpa Martin and asked him for money for our bus tickets. Believe it or not, he sent her the money. We got on the Greyhound bus and went to Yale, Oklahoma, and stayed for a little while. Aunt Tildie washed dishes in a cafe and I babysat children. We made enough money for a train ticket back home to Delaplaine, Arkansas.

We got home just in time that spring to chop cotton.

Grandpa told Aunt Tildie we had to pay him back for the bus tickets, so it took all the money we made that spring chopping cotton to pay him back.

I remember one day we went into Delaplaine, to visit Tom Hall's store, and Aunt Tildie was telling Ollie Hall how the only time her dad ever gave her any money, he wanted it back.

I also remember what Ms. Ollie said: "Walter Martin don't have a heart; he has a wart on his pounch" (meaning on his stomach).

We owed Grandpa thirty-four dollars each. It doesn't sound like much does it? But in 1949 it was a lot of money, since we got three dollars a day for chopping cotton ten hours.

In the years from 1945 until 1950, Grandpa would come down from Missouri in the fall to pick cotton. He would work all day, only stopping for a drink of water once in a while but never stopping for lunch. Sometimes Corrie would come with him, but she never picked cotton. She tried a time or two but could never pick enough to fill half a sack during a workday.

When I was a kid, my grandparents (Mama's parents) were the only people I knew who were divorced. Then, I didn't understand any of it. They were my grandparents, my mama's parents. That was the bottom line. Divorce wasn't discussed in front of children.

Joyce, Alma, Noma Lou, Don and our cousin Anna May Pitcher, 1950

Joyce, Eufa, Alma, 1952

Eufa's sister Betty (left) and Eufa, 1949

Laura Harlan (the preacher's daughter), Eufa and Eufa's little brother, Don, 1950

The Mulberry Bush

Here we go around the mulberry bush,
Here we go round the mulberry bush,
So early in the morning.

This is the way we chop our cotton,
This is the way we chop our cotton,
So early in the morning.

That is the way we sang that little song when I was a kid. I can't remember all the verses we made up about all the things we did going around the mulberry bush.

But I do remember a mulberry tree that grew on the old river bank when I was about twelve years old. Our cotton patch started at our front yard and ran down to the ditch dump; that was what we called the Cache River banks. Anyway, we were still chopping cotton the last part of June in 1945 or 1946. Bub, Betty, cousin Barbara, Aunt Tildie, and I chopped cotton as usual. It was so hot and we were tired and bored, those rows of cotton seemed to be getting longer by the minute. It was the middle of the morning and us kids were really slowing down. Aunt Tildie was getting way ahead of us. She was already halfway back down a row. Going back toward the house, she kept yelling for us to get busy and catch up; but we didn't pay much attention to her (we never did), which didn't make her a bit happy. I don't remember Mama or Daddy ever telling us we had to mind Aunt Tildie; she just assumed we were supposed to, and I guess Mama and Daddy just assumed we would.

But by the time we got to the end of the rows and to the river bank where the woods started, Aunt Tildie was almost back at our house. We heard some blue jays and squirrels out in the woods. They sounded like they were having a real party; so we laid our hoes down and went to investigate. They were having a party alright: there in the woods on the ditch dump was a mulberry tree; it was about twenty feet tall and twenty or twenty-five inches around and just covered with ripe mulberries. But the limbs were all too high for us to reach. The blue jays seemed to be laughing at us and the squirrels were cussing at us and telling us to GO AWAY, which we did. We started back toward the house, chopping cotton as fast as we could. By the time we got there it was almost noon. Mama had some lunch ready, so we ate and got to rest a little while. Then we had to chop cotton all that afternoon. That night it rained; so the next day it was too wet and muddy in the fields for us to chop cotton. We got the day off.

Now, back to the mulberries. We knew we couldn't reach them so Bub got Daddy's chopping ax and we headed to the river bank and the mulberry tree. We threw sticks at the squirrels and jaybirds. The birds tried to peck us on the head, but we were intent on getting our share of those berries, so we started chopping. Bub chopped awhile, then I chopped some more. It took awhile but the tree finally came crashing down. We ate mulberries until we were purple.

We played around on the riverbank and mulberry tree most of the day. When Mama finally called us to come to the house, we were a real purple mess. Mama asked Bub what he was doing with the chopping ax and he said, "Getting mulberries." Mom inquired, "With an ax?" Bub replied, "Yes, we had to chop the tree down to get them."

Mama wanted to know if we thought that was a very wise choice. She wanted to know if we thought there would be any berries on that tree come next spring. She said she wondered if the birds and squirrels thought we did a good thing. And that was our "whipping" for cutting down the mulberry tree.

Sure, the birds and squirrels would find another tree somewhere; but would we? Or some day would we find another Mulberry Party to go to?

Auntie-over, Cowboys and Indians

One of the games we played as children, "auntie-over," is played with a ball, not with your aunt. And it doesn't mean throwing her over the house!

When I went to Brownie School, we played this game. We selected two teams; it didn't matter how many kids were on each side, just so each side was equal. One team would be on one side of the schoolhouse, the other team would go to the opposite side. I don't remember which team got the ball first, but I don't think it mattered. The team with the ball would yell "auntie-over!" and throw the ball over the schoolhouse. The team on the other side would try to catch it. If they didn't catch it and the ball hit the ground, they had to yell "auntie-over!" and throw the ball back to the other team, who would then try to catch it. If they did catch the ball, they would run around to the other side and try to touch as many of the other team members as they could with the ball while the other team was running to the opposite side of the schoolhouse. If you touched any of them with the ball, they had to come be on your team, and so on, until one team wound up with the most players. That team was the winner.

Sometimes a bunch of the cousins and friends came to our house and we would play auntie-over, if we could find a ball to play with. Sometimes we would have to make a ball out of an old sock. To make a ball out of an old sock, you wrap a small rock or a green cotton boll in a lot of cotton, put it in the sock and tie it up. It was kind of hard to throw that over the house. You had to have a pretty strong throwing arm; but we had long strong arms from picking and chopping cotton all the time, not to mention pumping and carrying water.

A lot of times at school we played cowboys and Indians at recess and lunchtime. We would make our own guns and bows and arrows. Wooden guns and bows and arrows made from sticks and string didn't hurt anybody. I don't think we really knew what a cowboy or even an Indian was.

I remember going to a movie or two with Grandma and Orville. We would go to a place called Evening Star (about ten miles away) and a man would put up a tent and show old western movies with music. We paid a nickel to sit on a wooden bench in that tent and watch those old movies. They were usually silent ones. That turned into a game for us kids. We made our guns and bows and arrows, took them to school and played cowboys and Indians. Don't try doing that nowadays. I guess the reasons are obvious. Oh, how the time changes things and people.

We also got to listen to the stories about the Lone Ranger and Tonto on the radio. I now have on a CD, Rossini's "William Tell Overture." Sometimes when I am by myself, I play it and remember being a kid listening to the Lone Ranger. I can almost hear and see all us kids at the old one-room school running around the schoolhouse and big old oak trees playing at being cowboys and Indians. We also listened to stories of Superman. The radio program came on at four o'clock in the afternoon. Us kids would hurry home from school to listen to it. Sometimes we would get home and Daddy would be listening to a ballgame; we would be very disappointed (but we didn't say a word since that just wasn't done). We only had one radio and we were lucky to have that. It was an old battery-powered radio and a lot of the time the battery was run down and we couldn't buy another one until the fall when we picked cotton and earned more money.

Daddy loved to listen to baseball games, so he always tried to get a battery. Sometimes when we didn't have one we would walk up to Grandma and Orville's house and listen to the Grand Ole Opry on Saturday night. It was a half a mile walk, not bad going, but walking back in the dark when you were a kid and tired and sleepy wasn't much fun. But now it's a memory I don't want to ever forget.

Rural Electrification Comes to Kinfolks Island

From April until November, in the bottomlands of northeastern Arkansas, when I was growing up in the 1930s and 40s, we stayed outdoors as much as possible. One reason was that there wasn't much to do indoors and there wasn't room to do anything except eat and sleep. Two rooms ain't much for ten people; besides, it was too hot indoors. Even with all the flies and mosquitoes, it was better to be outside; the wind would keep the insects off you. Or you could build a bonfire with green limbs and grass and the smoke would drive them away, and it was cooler under a shade tree.

If you had school homework to do, you got it done before dark. The only light you had at night in your house was an ole kerosene lamp, usually with a smoky chimney. Did you ever have to clean kerosene lamp globes? Or put kerosene in oil lamps? I have more times than I care to remember. Anyway, if you had a light in the house after dark that was where the "skeeters" and little green harvest bugs went. Even if you had screens on the doors and windows those little bugs and mosquitoes would find a way to those lamps. You couldn't close the doors and windows or you would suffocate.

We went to bed when it got dark; it would be so hot and sticky we couldn't sleep. Sometimes we made pallets on the floor. It was cooler there than on the beds. We made fans from pieces of cardboard boxes or anything we could find that would stir up the hot humid air; even the "skeeters" didn't bite us so much. We were so sweaty I think the salt in the sweat killed them or they drowned in it. I don't think we went to sleep until about daylight when the air cooled down, if you could call 85 degrees and 100 percent humidity cool. I think we just fell unconscious from the heat and exhaustion from trying to fan ourselves. Daddy would be the first to wake up, if he had even been asleep. He would yell at everyone else until we came out of our heat-related comas.

I lived like this until I was sixteen, which was in 1949. All the people on Kinfolks Island and areas close by got together and signed something to get the Rural Electrification Administration to agree to bring the electric lines on across to our homes. From then on we were really into the Modern Ages. We had electric lights; bugs and mosquitoes really liked those.

We also got an electric window fan and an electric refrigerator. Daddy got it from the same place he had gotten the tractor: from the International Harvester Company. And he got Mama a Maytag washing machine: wringer type, of course. So you see, by that time we weren't living in the Dark Ages anymore. I was seventeen by then.

We still didn't have an indoor bathroom or running water. The only running water was what us kids got from the pump. Daddy said there wasn't going to be a toilet inside a house in which he lived and ate. And for as long as he lived there wasn't. Not even in the new house he built after I was married and moved to Oklahoma. My husband helped Daddy wire the new house for electricity. After Daddy passed away in 1961, Mama had a bathroom put in and an electric pump put on the new well right beside the house for cold running water. I'm not sure if she ever got a hot water heater. Years later she came to live with me.

Left to right: cousin Barbara, sister Betty, me (Eufa), cousin Josalee, sister Joyce, and sister Alma.
We had been swimming in the old Cache River drainage ditch. Gotta love our swim suits! 1947.

Cache River

Cache River drainage ditch was a large part of my life as a child. In fact, everyone who lived and tried to make a go of it in the Cache River bottomlands from the 1930s until the 1950s depended on the drainage ditch. We dealt with the overflow waters, the mud and mosquitoes for thirty or forty-odd years.

My daddy bought the forty acres of swampland in 1939 or 1940. He paid 235 dollars for it. He borrowed the money from the bank and paid it back forty-nine dollars a year, out of what we would make off the cotton crops.

Cache River cut a path across the east corner of our forty acres, that's why I'm always calling it the thirty-seven acre farm. The two old sloughs took up another two acres, and when it rained a lot they took up several more acres for months at a time. It wasn't all bad though. The overflow made the land real fertile; everything grew fast and vigorous when it didn't get flooded and washed away or mostly just drowned, because overflow water doesn't rush out all over, it just creeps out and slowly covers everything over.

When the river was down in its banks you could catch as many big buffalo and catfish as you wanted. As I said before, Daddy made part of our living by catching fish and selling them. He had big fishnets in the river, along with trotlines; that's how he caught so many big fish (that was when you were allowed to do that).

Before my time, or even my dad's time, the Cache River was just an old river and when it rained a lot, the water would rush down its course taking old dead trees and all kinds of debris, mud, and sand with it. Homes and farms along the river (which was all the lowland around Delaplaine and a little place called Light) would flood, because the old trees and stuff would get caught together in places in the river and cause dams and all the water to run out all over the land, into the old sloughs and make lagoons out of them. Of course a lot of fish and turtles would get caught in these sloughs when the river went back down in its banks.

When people started farming the bottomlands back in the early 1900s, or maybe even earlier, they decided to try to drain all the swampland. I think there was a judge who got the drainage started. They got an organization going called the Cache River Drainage Association. It dredged out the old river course as far as it could, because when it got to the next county the people there wouldn't let them go on through so the drainage thing didn't help all that much. Of course I didn't know all this stuff when I was a kid. All I knew was a lot of times the old river would overflow and drown the cotton plants and Daddy would have to plow and plant all over again. Some years this would occur so late in the growing season that the cotton wouldn't have time to make out very well, so of course we didn't make out very well either. Daddy would make ties for the railroad and sell fish to get us through the winter in hopes that in the next spring it wouldn't rain so much and overflow the river.

Sometimes in the summer the river would get real low and we could go swimming in it. But most of the time it was too deep and muddy and full of trash, snakes and mud turtles (big ones). In that old river and of course in the old sloughs too there were water moccasins as big and as long as my legs.

One summer, when I was about eleven or twelve years old, the water had been up and out all over the land in the spring. But during the summer there wasn't much rain and everything dried up, except the old slough down by the river on our farm. So us kids went there to fish. In this slough there was an enormous cypress stump; it was probably six feet tall and as big around as a large dining table. The heart of the old stump had rotted away, so there was a big hole there instead. And there was fish in it because stump was in the water and the hole was full of dark murky water. We made ourselves a foot-log from the bank out to the stump and walked out there and fished in that dark water. We caught some perch out, then we set out a pole and left it there. We thought we might catch a big catfish as we had got a glimpse of one down there in the dark water. We went to the house for a while. Late that afternoon we went back to see if we had caught anything. Well! We had, as the fishing line was jerking and the pole was moving. Bub and I went out on the foot-log to get it. We had an awful time getting our catch up out of that hole, and when we did, we didn't know what to do with it, nor did we know what it was we had caught. It was long and slick and black. We knew it wasn't a snake, at least not one we had ever seen the likes of. We sure did not want to touch it, or try to take it off the hook and line. We finally decided to drag it to the house to see if Mama knew what it was. Well! When she saw us dragging that thing she thought it was a snake. She started yelling at us, wanting to know "what in the world we thought we were doing." Daddy was home and came out the kitchen door, because by that time, that was where we were. Well, he didn't like the looks of our catch either. He said it was some kind of eel (I don't remember what he called it now). He told us not to touch it and for Bub to go get the chopping ax. No! we said. We were not going to have eel for supper. He chopped off its head and took it out in the woods where there was a brush pile and threw it on it.

This was probably the closest I've ever come to eating eel though.

I see it in supermarkets nowadays; but I sure wouldn't want to eat it. I remember Daddy saying it was poison.

There's no telling where that ole eel came from. The Cache River runs from north of Knob, Arkansas, northeast of Peach Orchard, to the White River at Clarendon, which is in the east central part of the state. That's about halfway across the eastern part of Arkansas.

My life has been a lot like that old Cache River, sometimes up and sometimes down, sometimes hitting snags and causing dams, but always finding a way to get through, always taking mainly the same course, just not the same path.

Jones Ridge Cemetery

Over from our little farm, about a mile and a half away, there is a ridge like some of the ones around our place and Uncle Isaac's. The ones us kids called hills. But this ridge is much larger. A lot of Indian artifacts have been found on this ridge. There is an old graveyard there that goes back to at least the 1880s and probably farther back because there are stones and markers that don't have names or dates left on them. It seemed like an old cemetery when I was a kid.

I found out the cemetery was named for a man named C. G. Jones. I suppose he must have owned the land at that time, and he was the County Treasurer back in 1852-1854.

A lot of people I knew when I was growing up are buried there. I have found out that is where my schoolteacher, Mrs. Vesta Varville from the old one-room school is buried.

When I was about twelve or thirteen, there was an old lady who lived about a half mile from the Brownie Schoolhouse. One of the farmers let her live in a little old house he owned. She lived by herself; she had no family that anyone knew of. I don't know where she came from and don't know if anyone else did. I can't even remember her name. Anyway, in the late spring, the old lady passed away, and there was no one to see about her funeral, so the neighbors got together to bury her.

Ms. Vesta had some of us girls bring flowers from our yards and wildflowers we picked along the road on our way to school. She let us sit on the schoolhouse porch and make wreaths, and one of the neighbors came by and took us girls and the wreaths to the old Jones Ridge Cemetery for the funeral for the old lady. It was just the close neighbors and us girls from school; there were four or five of us. When the grave was covered over the man from the funeral home had us girls lay the homemade wreaths on the grave. Being a twelve-year-old kid from a large family, it was sad and unreal to me that someone lived to be that old and had no one to mourn for her.

A couple of years later my dad got us kids a job picking cotton. Well, can you figure how I felt when he told us where we were going to work? It was for the people that farmed all the land around the Jones Ridge Cemetery.

It wasn't easy picking cotton and trying not to imagine seeing and hearing things when you would straighten up from bending over a row of cotton (you had to do this once in a while to let your back muscles straighten out) and you would be right by the graveyard.

Sometimes I would think I could see that old lady waving at me and smiling; I guessed it was because of the flowers.

We would find a lot of arrowheads in the area around the ridge when we were picking cotton for that farmer.

My dad said he thought where the cemetery was, used to be an Indian campground. He said that Indians had lived all around in the bottomlands long before, when it was all woods, rivers and old sloughs. Then the timber companies came and cut down a lot of the big trees. I guess that was why there were so many old cypress stumps, like the one where we caught the eel.

There was still a lot of forest all around in the bottomlands when I was a kid, though. My dad set traps to catch mink, beaver, raccoons and possums in the winter months, and sell the furs; but it got so they weren't worth much, so it didn't pay to do that. Besides, by the time I was grown so much of the forest had been cut down to make room for farms, the animals didn't thrive there as well, not anything like they did when the Indians were there, I'm sure, or even like it was for the French fur traders when they were there also.

Once my dad found an Indian tomahawk; but we didn't keep it, as a man came along and wanted it and said he would put it in a museum. We never really knew if he did or not; he may have just wanted it for his own collection.

We never talked much about Indian stuff. Back then if you had a lot of Indian heritage, you didn't talk about it. I think Mama and her sisters might have been afraid that they would get sent back to Oklahoma and would have to live on the reservation or something; you see that was where they were born: Oklahoma, not the reservation. There's no telling what my Grandpa Martin had told them when they were growing up. I know they had a lot of very different ideas about a lot of things. They thought if you looked and acted in a certain way and kept quiet, things would be OK. And I guess they were—for no more than I knew as a kid.

Flowers of the Field

Seems like kids are always hungry, or just looking for something to eat. I know my grandkids are always holding the refrigerator door open and if I ask them what they want, they just say, "I'm just looking."

Well, that is similar to what it was like when I was a kid myself sixty years ago, with a few exceptions. One being, we had no refrigerator, not until I was about sixteen.

Our snack bar and refrigerator was the garden, or in the winter, it was the barn and smokehouse where we had stored stuff from the garden and fields.

In the fall we could find food just about everywhere: in the cotton patch, the cornfield, and what was left of the garden. And we could find food in the woods all around the fields. We always planted peas and watermelons in the cornrows with the corn so in the fall we could still find ripe melons. We could take a break in mid-morning from picking cotton, find a watermelon, take it to a shade tree at the end of our cotton rows and have a snack, wipe our mouth and hands on a handful of cotton, stick our dirty cotton napkin in our pick-sack and go back to work.

In the woods close to the cotton fields grew a lot of possum grapevines. The grapes on these were ripe in the fall also. In the woods were many, many, hickory trees for the grapevines to climb on, and many hickory nuts to eat as well. It was hard to find anything to crack the nuts with however, as there weren't many rocks in the bottomlands.

Around the edges of the fields and sometimes in the cotton rows, vines of all kinds grew. Some were like poison ivy; I didn't like those. But there was one vine that had pretty lilac and purple blooms and in the fall they turned into big oval shaped green balls; then the balls would turn a light yellowish green. We would peel and eat the fleshy parts from around seed. I didn't know what they were then. I just knew it was all right to eat them because mom said it was. I now know they were passion flower fruits.

Persimmon was "another favorite," but we had to wait until after the first frost to eat them or your mouth wouldn't come un-puckered till Christmas.

When we would walk home just before nightfall, we would go by our turnip patch, pull up a big fat turnip, wipe the dirt off it on our britches leg, and munch on that as we walked home.

Sometimes if we felt brave enough, we would go through Uncle Isaac and Aunt Jessie's apple orchard and swipe a few apples. They didn't like us doing that very much, but couldn't say too much since cousin Barbara was right there with us.

In the spring, we could hardly wait until we saw the first shoots of green poke salad stalks peeking up around old brush piles and along the edges of the woods and barn lots. Mama and us kids would go out picking greens; there were lots of lambs quarter, narrow dock, and wild mustard, all of these things together made a very good salad.

We would walk through the woods between our house and my grandmother's and pick bouquets of wild Sweet Williams. I can still smell them today (in my mind). There was also what we called sheep-showers. It was really sheep-sorrel. We would eat the little purple-green sour leaves.

I could never get my kids to eat poke salad greens and my grandchildren won't touch them with a ten-foot pole, let alone a fork. They say they are not eating no under-brush!

Who do you think would have a better chance of survival in the wild? A kid raised like I was? Or a kid who opens the refrigerator door and can't find anything they want to eat? But they are always hungry.

The churchhouse we built between our place and Delaplaine, Arkansas. Uncle Isaac and Aunt Jessie, 1949.

A group of people going to church, 1946. The big man was the first preacher we had, Brother Bob Burge.

Delaplaine, Arkansas, Population 243

When I was a kid, Delaplaine, Arkansas, was "Town." It was three miles from where we lived on Kinfolks Island; where our thirty-seven acre farm was, and still is today. My brother Bub still owns it, or his wife Barbara does, as my brother passed away a few years ago. His son, Tony Eubanks, still farms it; only now soybeans and rice grow there.

No more cotton patches. No one picks cotton by hand any more, that I know about. Everything is done with machines.

Delaplaine is in Green County in northeastern Arkansas. It is about thirty-five miles west of Jonesboro, Arkansas, and it is not very far from Jonesboro to West Memphis, Tennessee. But when I was a kid, those places might as well have been on the moon, as we never went to them, either. Delaplaine and Paragould were as far from the cotton patches as we got. Maybe we went to Walnut Ridge and Pocahontas once in a blue moon.

The only way we got to go anywhere back then was in an old steel-tired wagon pulled by a team of old plow horses or ole balky mules, whichever Daddy owned at the time.

At that time, Delaplaine consisted of Ira and Ollie Hall's grocery and dry goods store; the post office, run by Mr. Bill Clayton, the postmaster; and the drug store, run by Dr. Hutchens (Doc Hutch), he was the doctor and the druggist.

Of course there was the cotton gin, which was on the other side of the railroad tracks from the grocery store and drugstore.

At times we had a cafe, run by different people at different times. Seems like the only time it was open was during cotton picking season. That was the only time people had enough money to eat anywhere besides home and then it was mostly men who ate there after they got their cotton wagons unloaded and got the money from their bales of cotton.

Also the big school was there: Delaplaine High School, which is still there today. I started school there when I was six; didn't go very long until we moved over to the thirty-seven acre farm, then I got to go to Brownie, the one-room school. I went there until I was about fifteen, then I went back to Delaplaine High for two years. I finally got through the eighth grade.

My Grandpa Eubanks was the Justice of the Peace at Delaplaine for a long time, in later years. Rual Harpole was the sheriff. His brother James was sheriff too, part of the time, I think. Maybe they took turns. They also drove the school buses for Delaplaine School. James's wife, Mrs. Nellie, was one of the teachers.

Delaplaine High School was built in 1938 by the men working for the WPA. So it was a new school when I went there in 1939 for the short time.

The year I graduated from the eighth grade, we were told that the next year we would have to buy our own schoolbooks. I thought I couldn't do that and buy my clothes too. And Daddy said he didn't have the money to buy books, so that was the end of that. One of the teachers, Mr. Emil Thomas, tried to get me to stay in school; but being a sixteen-year-old girl, I thought I had to have clothes like the other girls or I couldn't go. I know now that I should have gone on to school and gotten an education and risen above the environment and made different circumstances for myself and probably others also. I know when you are a kid you really don't think of things like that; especially if no one ever talks to you about it.

None of my family was educated, except maybe Grandpa Eubanks. I've heard my mom say she had a third grade education and Daddy had about the same, so they never attached much importance to schooling, especially for girls. So Delaplaine and me are about the same as we were sixty or seventy years ago. I lived and did what was expected of me, I guess. I got married when I was nineteen, had and raised five children, have fifteen grandkids, and two great grandchildren. Otherwise, I haven't done anything toward changing the world, or making things any better for myself or anyone else.

Delaplaine is still the same little town as it was then, only there is no more cotton gin, and most of the Hall family I knew are gone. Kinfolks Island has changed a little (Cache River doesn't overflow so much, as the people got it dug on through to where it was supposed to be in the place). The island is still mostly owned by kinfolks though. No kids pick cotton. Sometimes I think things would be better if they were picking cotton.

I don't feel bad about the way I was raised. My parents did the best they knew how considering the way things were sixty and seventy years ago.

It seems like my life has gone from the dark ages to the computer age (or high tech). Like from kerosene lamps and wood cook stoves, to push button lights and microwaves; steel-tired wagons and mules to jet planes and rockets to the moon.

It's kinda hard for an old brain to keep up with the changes. My fifteen-year-old grandson can take a VCR apart, fix it, and put it together again. When I was fifteen I didn't know how to make a long distance phone call. My grandkids have e-mail addresses and fax machines.

THEN AND NOW

Windmills and cartwheels
Hot air balloons
Bicycles and go-carts
Old radio tunes
A stroll by the river
A walk in the park
Playing baseball all day
Counting stars after dark
Fresh air and sunshine
Clear running streams
A day full of laughter
And nights full of dreams
Our feet on the ground
The sky up above
Our minds were at peace
Our hearts filled with love

Why has our world changed so much?

Computers and e-mail
Telephone and fax
Is your neighbor your neighbor?
Don't turn your back
Fast cars and four lanes
Nuclear power
A hundred miles we go
in less than an hour.
Air filled with smog
Lakes filled with grime
The only thing growing
is Taxes and crime.
Cheat on your neighbor
Lie to your friend
Life doesn't matter
So when will it end?
We must slow down, start protecting our natural world.
When it is gone; so are we.

—A poem by my baby sister, Noma Lou Eubanks-Snider

About the Author

Eufa Eubanks-Adkison lives in the small town of Bakersfield in the Ozark hills of Missouri, with her husband of fifty years. They have five grown children who all live within a fifty-mile radius of them.

She has always loved to read and write. She is mostly self-educated, and received her G.E.D. at age fifty-five. She wrote these childhood stories over a period of five years.

Ms Eubanks-Adkison wants everyone to know how important it is to have an education no matter how young or how old you are, or under what circumstances you may live.